perspectives
ON DESIGN
pacific northwest

design philosophies expressed by the pacific northwest's leading professionals

Published by

PANACHE
P A N A C H E   P A R T N E R S

Panache Partners, LLC
1424 Gables Court
Plano, TX 75075
469.246.6060
Fax: 469.246.6062
www.panache.com

Publishers: Brian G. Carabet and John A. Shand

Printed in Malaysia

Distributed by Independent Publishers Group
800.888.4741

PUBLISHER'S DATA

Perspectives on Design Pacific Northwest

Library of Congress Control Number: 2009932105

ISBN 13: 978-1-933415-61-1
ISBN 10: 1-933415-61-4

First Printing 2010

10 9 8 7 6 5 4 3 2 1

Right: Shugart Bates, page 41

Previous Page: Vandeventer + Carlander Architects, page 61

Panache Partners, LLC, is dedicated to the restoration and conservation
of the environment. Our books are manufactured using paper from
mills certified to derive their products from well-managed forests. We
are committed to continued investigation of alternative paper products
and environmentally responsible manufacturing processes to ensure the
preservation of our fragile planet.

perspectives
ON DESIGN
pacific northwest

design philosophies expressed by the pacific northwest's leading professionals

introduction

SkB Architects, page 51

E. Cobb Architects, page 11

Creating the spaces in which we live and achieving the beauty we desire can be a daunting quest—a quest that is as diverse as each of our unique personalities. For some, it may be serene hardscaped gardens, for others it may be opulent marble entryways. Aspiring chefs may find a kitchen boasting the finest in technology their true sanctuary.

Perspectives on Design Pacific Northwest is a pictorial journey, from conceptualizing your dream home, to putting together the finishing touches, to creating an outdoor oasis. Alongside the phenomenal photography, you will have a rare insight to how these tastemakers achieve such works of art and be inspired by their personal perspectives on design.

Within these pages, the region's finest artisans will share their wisdom, experience and talent. It is the collaboration between these visionaries and the outstanding pride and craftsmanship of the products showcased that together achieve the remarkable. Learn from leaders in the industry about the aesthetics of a finely crafted sofa, or how appropriate lighting can dramatically change the appearance of a room.

Whether your dream is to have a new home or one that has been redesigned to suit your lifestyle, *Perspectives on Design Pacific Northwest* will be both an enjoyable journey and a source of motivation.

Steve Jensen, page 263

contents

E. Cobb Architects, page 11

Shugart Bates, page 41

the concept

chapter one

Jeffrey Lamb at V3 Studio, page 31   SkB Architects, page 51   Vandeventer + Carlander Architects, page 61

One hundred years ago, the architect Adolf Loos postulated the criminal nature of ornament in architecture: Ornament is excess and a source of fleeting style. Eric Cobb founded his firm on a pair of guiding principles that search for timelessness in design and sculptural assemblies of raw materials.

E. Cobb Architects' first principle is elevating structure and the basic building assemblies to finished surfaces. Conventional buildings typically use their "skin," both interior and exterior, as their primary expressive opportunities. Instead, the team prioritizes the role of the actual structure over that of the skin. True structural members and simple, honest assemblies define how structures perform. This is the body of the architectural design. No fakery, no ornament.

The second principle is searching beyond conventional boundaries for the most complete design solutions. Strong design solutions are then woven across disciplines, creating unique experiences tailored to site and user. Often this involves the close collaboration of a special group of consultants, including landscape architect Bruce Hinckley, structural engineer Jim Harriott and interior designer Elizabeth Stretch. The resultant structures are highly functional, modern, understandable and, above all, genuine.

"Something fantastic happens when structure, space and finish become one thing."

—Eric Cobb

E. COBB ARCHITECTS

"How a building and structure perform becomes inseparable from the design."

—Eric Cobb

RIGHT: We stripped back everything in the condominium to expose the sand-blasted concrete structure. Natural light was filtered through aluminum bar grating suspended beneath a skylight for an even distribution of light. We inserted a few carefully placed walls to be surfaces for art as well as spatial dividers. The table is a single, monolithic slab of wood, 22 feet long.
Photograph by Steve Keating Photography

PREVIOUS PAGES LEFT: By the time you've reached the front door, you feel that you're already inside the house. By engaging the landscape with the architecture very deliberately, we've created a subtle layering of unique moments, each closer to the interior of the house. Next to the dark cantilevered concrete porch, a steel rail is cut back to its essence, and you are fully embraced at the entry. The actual door is a formality.
Photograph by Paul Warchol, Warchol Photography

PREVIOUS PAGES RIGHT: The great room is a demonstration of the honest materials that create the structure. The wooden beams are the roof structure. Custom steel connections allow the beams themselves to be the primary expression, controlling the aesthetic of each connection. Heated concrete slabs create the floor. These simple materials are elevated to a high level of finish, where they themselves become the design.
Photograph by Paul Warchol, Warchol Photography

"By minimizing ornament, you can find the true bones."

—Eric Cobb

TOP: The stage of an old, refurbished auditorium became the second level to the condominium and flows into the kitchen to become the countertop. The cantilevered stair treads and the floor surface are the same terrazzo material but with contrasting color. The charcoal gray treads become sculptural objects against the white background.

BOTTOM: Outside the master bedroom door, a part vestibule, part library links and separates the private spaces to the public spaces. The second-story library with glass floor is served by a steel ladder. The space between each rung is a frame for small artwork.

FACING PAGE: From the entry, the rest of the condominium is separated by a screen. Beyond, the original concrete structure is rediscovered and allowed to speak for itself.
Photographs by Steve Keating Photography

"By not clearly defining rooms as such, adjacent spaces engage each other, creating spectacular, surprising conditions with flowing space."

—Eric Cobb

ABOVE: A series of wooden boxes became the essential design. This "supersized cabinetry" contains all of the storage needs for the condominium. In the kitchen, we chose to slip the basalt countertops off the boxes, cantilevered to make special conditions for display. These stone slabs become loose objects in the space, separate from the wooden boxes.

FACING PAGE: The structure is a compositional study of a light-weight wooden vessel and its relationship to a concrete block foundation. The two are intentionally misaligned and loosely fitted to create cantilevered decks, a volumetric play, and interesting spaces between them.
Photographs by Paul Warchol, Warchol Photography

"We try to extend our efforts well beyond the conventional elements of architecture."

—Eric Cobb

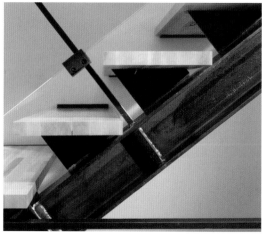

ABOVE LEFT: Wood can be very powerful. The ceiling is a series of exposed glue-laminated beams. The structure is the complete finished ceiling. The fireplace is cast-in-place concrete, while the suspended steel lighting structure lights the wood ceiling above and the conversation area below. The asymmetrical composition of elements creates a comfortable, informal living space.
Photograph by Paul Warchol, Warchol Photography

ABOVE RIGHT: The stair contrasts a raw steel stringer with highly finished wood treads. No risers, no trim: no excess.
Top photograph by Eric Cobb
Bottom photograph by Steve Keating Photography

FACING PAGE LEFT: An elevated, cantilevered bedroom is supported by an exposed steel frame. The cantilever supports the bedroom but defines a protected outdoor space below it.
Photographs by Paul Warchol, Warchol Photography

FACING PAGE RIGHT: To replace a long, steep run of stairs down to the home, we installed a nautical bridge directly to the top floor of the house, keeping you high and light. Inside, a dramatic steel stair descends to the great room.
Photograph by Chris Eden

Jim Graham and Brett Baba are creative visionaries of residential architecture. By first considering the lives of the individuals who inhabit their buildings, they understand the importance of evolving this direct relationship. Elements such as the definition between public and private spaces, prominence of indoor-outdoor connections and even the floorplan evolve out of a nuanced understanding of tastes, habits and routines.

Graham Baba Architects incorporates sustainability and the most advanced technologies into each design and always demands the finest in workmanship. The unique character and topography of the building site inform the fundamental nature of the orientation, design and choice of materials. Graham Baba's progressive yet elegant work demonstrates the effectiveness of open communication, a talented design team and close ties with talented artisans, fabricators and craftspeople.

"Coming up with good ideas is never the issue. It's distilling those ideas down to the essence that is crucial."

—Jim Graham

GRAHAM BABA ARCHITECTS

ABOVE & FACING PAGE: As we designed and planned the remodel, we drew inspiration from a traditional Japanese farmhouse aesthetic. Materials such as bamboo and steel are celebrated in their natural state, and various design elements are thoughtfully layered for a clean yet well-developed expression. To create privacy without losing the warmth of sunlight, we used industrial fiberglass panels so the windows would read like rice-paper shoji screens.
Above & facing page bottom photographs by Benjamin Benschneider
Facing page top photographs by Michael Matisse

PREVIOUS PAGES: Honesty of structure is extremely important in our work. We peeled back the plastered fireplace to reveal the original brick at the fireplace, a wonderful relic of the past that adds instant warmth to the space. The brick column in the living room is an old chimney that we preserved as an ordering element. We specified the steel columns with rivets at eye-level to add interest and express the detail of the connection. The home has a beautifully articulated ceiling, and the hip roof appears to have a deep overhang but it's actually less than 12 inches, an implied look.
Photographs by Benjamin Benschneider

"Architecture is an opportunity to express people's nuances in an exciting way."

—Brett Baba

RIGHT: The open pavilion is where life happens. And because the owners wanted their home to have a strong connection to the water, we oriented all of the seating areas to the wall of windows and kept the material palette organic. The quirky stools at the dining table express the casual nature of the space, an effect that is furthered by the buffet divider. We worked with fabricators to salvage pieces of metal—from unlikely things like a car hood, a washing machine and a furnace—and embrace their naturally weathered state to create a unique focal point.

Photograph by Benjamin Benschneider

"The subtlety of how materials meet is just as important as the overall architectural parti."

—Jim Graham

ABOVE & FACING PAGE: Spread out over three stories, the home's 5,400 square feet are well utilized. Beside the boat garage on the lower level, expansive glass doors slide into the wall for true indoor-outdoor living; the second level is the main living space, which has floor-to-ceiling glass; on the top floor, bedrooms enjoy total privacy and panoramic views. Cedar, reclaimed Australian gumwood and steel details are incorporated in various ways throughout the home, creating interest as well as continuity.

Above & facing page top photographs by Benjamin Benschneider

Facing page bottom photographs by Michael Matisse

"You never know where you'll find inspiration."
—Brett Baba

ABOVE: Open volumes are the key to making small spaces live large. We used walls sparingly to divide public and private uses in the sun-drenched, loft-like home. The fireplace element is clad in raw steel sheet to express as a vertical element and introduce a dark natural finish.

FACING PAGE: A home does not have to be prohibitively expensive to be unique and successful. It is about proportion, composition, scale and a solid understanding of craft and construction. The exposed ceiling framing helps zone the large open room, gives a sense of a taller ceiling height and introduces natural wood to the otherwise stark ceiling plane. Though the project's parameters limited the grade of windows we could select, our design gives the standard-sized windows a tailored look—and the aesthetic is nice and clean. The homeowner was intimately involved in developing the bright color palette; the green wall nicely accentuates the protruding bay with slot windows on either side. As a whole, the space reads as asymmetrical yet balanced, lighthearted yet classic, and far exceeds all expectations.
Photographs by Michael Matisse

Homebuilding, in its essence, is solving design problems. For Jeffrey Lamb, principal of V3 Studio, decades of experience have given the invaluable ability to decipher interior design elements. This functions across all genres; even the most innovative, modern homes are purely a creation of vigilant consideration of what is being worked with and who it is being worked for. The result is that his consistent immersion into specialized design has garnered much critical acclaim. In the ever-expanding globalization of the world, Jeffrey finds himself applying this principle internationally, and project size does not matter.

As the modern lifestyle moves closer toward condo living, the art of display becomes definitive. Jeffrey's theatrical background has taught him the importance of drama in spaces and that lighting is fundamentally important. Spaces often should be transparent, their function obvious yet intriguing. Being attuned to the infinite variety of materials means that Jeffrey and his V3 Studio team capture aesthetics through understanding. Mixed-use to residential, highrise to house, interiors to furniture, the projects that Jeffrey Lamb at V3 Studio takes on are typically provocative and consistently interesting.

"Interpretation of lifestyle is where a good design is born."

—Jeffrey Lamb

JEFFREY LAMB AT V3 STUDIO

> "Ideas should be tangible, so turning them into a reality is essential."
>
> —Jeffrey Lamb

ABOVE & FACING PAGE: Interiors always ask a question of lighting. In the master bathroom, red light floods the shower from a cast-glass window—natural elements are very important to counteract industrial elements like the stainless-steel water-heater casing. The ice cube-inspired, ADA bathroom becomes an interesting sculpture as light occurs within a double shell of frosted glass. And the stairwell is underlit so that entrance into the master suite is guided along a jutting wall of art.

PREVIOUS PAGES: I determined very quickly that the homeowner, an industrialist with a world-famous art collection, had a lifestyle of entertaining. I spent two days in the space, staying up all night, to devise an idea that would connect the industry of fabrication to his home, which also functions as a commercial space for an art gallery. The industrial aesthetic called for wood, steel, stone and glass, and he needed spaces that were private and compartmentalized—the 5,000-pound door shuts off the commercial side. No one had done glass stairs at this time, a very risky move that worked perfectly. The whole space is an engineering marvel.
Photographs by Richard Strode Photography

"Consistency is achieved through understanding."

—Jeffrey Lamb

RIGHT: Because of the varying works of art, the owner required a space that could function as a display for the big and small pieces. By cantilevering shelving off the wall, the entrance into the home becomes an art gallery, immersed in warm, African woods.
Photograph by Richard Strode Photography

FACING PAGE: For a penthouse overlooking the Columbia River, we asked the question: How many ways can we use this space? Taking out every wall we could, we took a philosophical approach to achieve enormous flexibility. Few things touch the floor or ceiling, which creates a floating sensation. Everything is changeable; the wall on which the central painting hangs spins to reveal a 60-inch television. But there is warmth in the well-crafted residence. Heavy on wood elements, the space minimizes its use of stone and glass. The Americana artifacts are right at home here.
Top photographs by Jeffrey Lamb
Bottom photograph by Richard Strode Photography

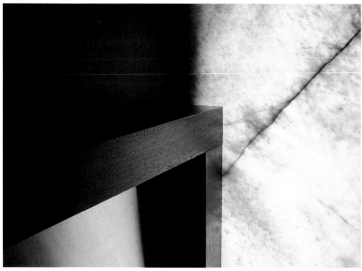

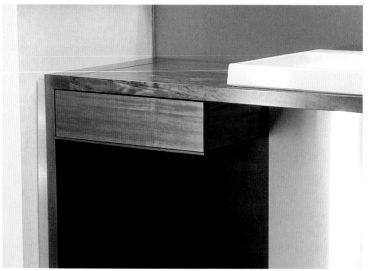

"Every great project builds on the next one—always with the same rigor."

—Jeffrey Lamb

RIGHT & FACING PAGE: The lifestyle of a doctor plays heavily in the home's design. For days straight, he may be working, followed by several days of sleeping. But the in-between moments are filled with entertaining. Because of the condo's positioning, it is one of the least private in the area, so to combat this on the doctor's downtime, sliding panels shut out the windows, cocooning the entire house in darkness. But when open, the windows maximize natural lighting in a practically voyeuristic fashion. At night, the bar has an illuminating effect. Steel beams across the ceiling hold lighting cans and speakers throughout—the system is very theatrical. I designed all of the furniture to go with the motif of translucent stone—backlit onyx creates mesmerizing lighting effects.

Right & facing page top photographs by Richard Strode Photography
Facing page bottom photographs by Jeffrey Lamb

"Detail and craft are the keys to good execution."

—Jeffrey Lamb

LEFT & FACING PAGE: The ninth-floor penthouse is a great exploration in large, open volumes. Areas are defined within the larger volumes by careful lighting and good furniture, all of which I designed. Drop areas get lighting to enunciate important spaces while the powder room exists as a highly crafted, translucent cube. The owner has a remarkable collection of music, and the penthouse is the perfect metaphor for this love since the home is truly a symphony of parts.

Photographs by Richard Strode Photography

Whether the professionals of Shugart Bates are designing a private residence, multifamily housing development, retail establishment or place of worship, their approach is the same: holistic, site-specific and guided by the clients' goals and dreams. The breadth of projects they undertake—from small-scale interior design work to large-scale master planning—enriches their process and expands their base knowledge. While the team enjoys the diversity of their commissions, they are admittedly partial to residential design, as no other project affords the same level of personal interaction.

Developing real relationships with clients is such a priority that the principals of Shugart Bates only accept projects for clients with whom they click, clients who are eager to be active participants in the creative process. From a single point of inspiration—derived from the client's desires and the site's offerings—the architects begin collaborating and exploring a range of possibilities. Through their approachable, design-based process, they dream big and then distill grand ideas to sound concepts that are equal parts relevant, durable, timeless and reflective of the owners' lifestyles.

"Great works of architecture are borne of an enlightened, collaborative process."

—Charlie Shugart

SHUGART BATES

RIGHT: Before we begin any design work, we spend a considerable amount of time getting to know our clients, understanding the future residents' needs and wants, surveying the site and defining project goals. From there, it is pure collaboration. We look to both the land and our clients for inspiration. Springboards for creativity can come from anywhere: tangible things like photographs, artwork or souvenirs; concepts like waves meeting the shoreline, the contour of the land, a family's history, travels and traditions. In creating Harvey House, which is nestled into the foothills of the Cascades and enjoys uninhibited views of Tiger Mountain, we drew inspiration from the family's love of art and music and their requests for "an uncommon use of common materials, splendor of the ordinary and a surprise around every corner"—not to mention the incredible site.

PREVIOUS PAGES: Our design responds to the natural setting in form and material composition. The roofline is an interpretation of the mountains' rugged qualities, each surface sloping a different degree and direction from the next, creating movement and interest. The use of natural and industrial materials—cedar siding, stucco, metal and concrete—gives the home an appealing "urban loft in the mountains" aesthetic. Blended into the roof forms are solar water-heating tubes, a green addition that complements the radiant-heated floors within. As the roof forms and massing imply, the residence is composed of three interconnected living units that afford privacy for the master suite in the east wing and the office and guest suite in the west wing; the first floor of the central unit contains the living, dining and kitchen areas.

Photographs by Steve Keating Photography

"The site and the people who will live there are the best sources of inspiration."

—Charlie Shugart

ABOVE & FACING PAGE: While we were conceptualizing the home, we came across an airplane magazine and decided that an airplane hangar door would be the perfect creative way to promote an indoor-outdoor lifestyle. The steel-framed glass wall is an impressive 12 feet tall by 17 feet wide. We furthered the interior-exterior connection through southern light-buffering overhangs that pass through the wall and terminate as the support for a light fixture over the dining table—the whimsical touch echoes the residents' fun-loving character.
Photographs by Steve Keating Photography

ABOVE & FACING PAGE: The wife is a garden design artist and sculptor; the husband is an engineer by profession and bassist in a local jazz band by passion; their two sons likewise have creative interests. We reflected the family's artistic inclinations in the architectural design as well as in the interior detailing. Blown-glass light fixtures and sculptures created by one of the sons combined with ornamental metalwork created by a family friend flow throughout the home. In the eastern wing, an artist's loft connects to the master bedroom, both of which have breathtaking mountain views.
Photographs by Steve Keating Photography

"Architecture is a holistic endeavor."

—Charlie Shugart

RIGHT & FACING PAGE: The main living areas have gracious ceiling heights and open layouts. Wherever possible, we designed spaces to be multifunctional, flexible in their uses. The kitchen, for instance, has a floating island that can easily be repositioned; the house works as a backdrop to the task at hand. Harvey House gave us the opportunity to create far more than architecture; we created a truly unique home that speaks to the artistic passions of its residents and daily elevates the quality of their family life.
Photographs by Steve Keating Photography

A good design is the solution to all building problems. Any firm that has a foot in building must, therefore, focus on innovation and creativity to find perfect solutions that meet homeowner and context needs. SkB Architects was founded on the principle that the effort to stay fresh keeps excitement at high levels for all involved. Headed by three architects, Shannon Rankin, Kyle Gaffney and Brian Collins-Friedrichs, the firm considers itself somewhat of a brain trust, blending the individual skills of the team members to produce unique end conditions.

SkB Architects is known for creating homes that support varied uses and lifestyles through an internal effort to understand new materials, which results in nontraditional experiments with windows, walls, roofing systems; by having architecture and interior design under the same roof, the team is better able to work with homeowners through full-service operations. With a triumvirate of skilled architects at its forefront, SkB Architects solves problems the old-fashioned way: with talent.

"We are all connected to nature—why not express that?"

—Shannon Rankin

SkB Architects

"You have to find rhythm.
Balance and harmony are
always correct answers."

—Brian Collins-Friedrichs

RIGHT: Homes that border Lake Washington usually have steeply sloped sites. Since the site allowed for a lower house, the streetside is low and discreet while the backside is intentionally grand to support the impressive views. Because of the volume of entertaining done by the homeowners, the courtyard—the public space—feels almost outside, pushing for a strong but quiet connection to the land. The angled roof also brings in natural light. But that is not to say that the home is all public spaces; private spaces can be found in multiple locations, such as the dining room, just below the treehouse-like master bedroom.
Photograph by John Granen

PREVIOUS PAGES: The owner of a lake house preferred not to spend his budget on square footage but rather on the right places. Keeping at a modest 3,500 square feet, the design focused on maximizing a compact, steep-slope site, using height to look out over the lake and maximizing spacious interior. With Mount Rainier in the distance, the home responds to the lightness, the airiness, the openness of its connection to nature. Since the irregular site boundary requires the entrance to slope upward, forcing the residents to come down into the home, the lake façade opens up, a practical view-finder with a metal exterior—a patinaed steel grating across a rusted steel wall. The roof is cantilevered up to augment the views.
Photographs by Benjamin Benschneider

ABOVE LEFT: Volume can sometimes be tricky. To make a two-story condominium grander, we used floor-to-ceiling drapery, seeking a hospitality quality for drama. Because of the narrowness of the room, the process was a bit like designing a ship. We wanted mobile-like lighting and found the perfect pendant fixture—basically a light sculpture—from Tom Dixon.
Photograph by John Granen

ABOVE RIGHT: A general contractor wanted to show some of his craft with steel in the architecture of his home. The three-story concrete wall—a single pour—had a massive aesthetic weight, and so we needed to contrast this with something fluid and organic. We designed a steel and bronze stair with a glass shield that would showcase the owner's work. The glass is set so that the rhythm in the ribbon steel would remain light, airy and fluid, never fighting for attention.
Photograph by Benjamin Benschneider

FACING PAGE: We designed the living room to play up the contrast of warm concrete and cool steel. The owners wanted a very tactile experience, so we floored the room in cast polished concrete, specified steel columns and structural beams and used a wood underbelly for the ceiling. The fireplace is clad in steel with a hearth and mural of precast concrete. Though the blending of materials and the structural design are very modern architectural examples, the home possesses an undeniable warmth and coziness, exemplifying harmony.
Photograph by John Granen

ABOVE: We restored an old, 1920s' office for an urban condo. Because of the amount of entertaining done in the penthouse, the guest bathroom was an important public space. With room for four or five people, the room even includes a large lounge chair. The walls are made of salvaged mirror pieces to mimic the tree-like candelabras atop the sink/credenza.

FACING PAGE: In the restoration, we needed to create an atmosphere perfect for entertaining. Since the company volume would be high, we designed the L-shaped nub for movement. To open the space a bit, we fabricated a sunroof by cutting in and installing blue lighting—urban codes disallowed a sunroof to cut all the way through. As it is in entertaining homes, the kitchen is truly the heart of the project.

Photographs by Eric Laignel

"A collective energy is the best fuel to get results."
—Kyle Gaffney

ABOVE: The dining table is a slab reclaimed from an old building. We sent the homeowners antiquing to find pieces that spoke to them—each of the dining room chairs is different, just as each guest enriches the conversation with his or her own unique life experiences. The room is warm, tactile and textured.

FACING PAGE: When the residents entertain, they can shut off the office with an old fire door, cut and reframed to fit a steel pipe. The leg of the kitchen counter was also taken from an old building and refurbished—both the top and leg are from a reclaimed beam from one of the client's existing buildings. We always look for great opportunities to cleverly repurpose pieces of history.
Photographs by Eric Laignel

andeventer + Carlander Architects has built a distinguished body of work in its first 10 years of practice. In 1998 Bill Vandeventer and Tim Carlander recognized that the synergy of their talents would create a solid base of expertise from which they could pursue architecture based on design excellence. Whereas both architects note that "it has not been easy," their commitment and dedication to their clients and the art of architecture has never wavered. Having been honored with numerous local and international design awards, they strive in every project to create an innovative architectural solution founded in the unique qualities inherent in every project.

The firm's approach is based on appropriateness while emphasizing architectural detail and the exploration of materials. Utilizing simple and elegant forms of modernism, projects are sensitive to site and context. While integrity of architectural concept and attention to client needs are readily evident in their work, homes designed by Vandeventer + Carlander Architects transcend sheer functionality and elevate the human spirit.

"Exploring and maximizing the creative potential of every project requires close collaboration with homeowners."

—Bill Vandeventer

VANDEVENTER + CARLANDER ARCHITECTS

"Pursuing the ideals of clarity and cohesiveness as manifested in the architectural concept unifies each design into a whole."

—Tim Carlander

RIGHT: Continuing a long and distinguished history of floating homes in Seattle, this new floating home is located on Lake Union in the heart of the city. The clients requested a contemporary home that would provide for comfortable living and gracious entertaining. Given a limited allowable footprint and the desire on the part of the owners to maximize both interior living and outdoor entertaining spaces, the plan flips the typical residential model by locating living spaces on the upper level and bedrooms on the entry level. This strategy allows for the consolidation of the upper floor into one large great room with direct access by circular stair to a rooftop deck. The design promotes flexibility of use and affords maximum exposure to views and light for all rooms in the home.

PREVIOUS PAGES LEFT: The conceptual design of the Madison Park residence is the resolution of the challenges and opportunities presented by the project site, the owner's program and budget and an architectural exploration of form, material and function. The goal was to achieve a synthesized design that meets the needs of the client while also investigating how a residence's architecture can be tested and transformed using new building technologies, materials and methods.

PREVIOUS PAGES RIGHT: The massing of the house is an exercise in carving; the challenge was to meet the clients' needs for space yet develop an envelope that is visually interesting and coherent. Various decks are recessed into the volume, and changes in materials and surfaces provide accents that speak to differentiated interior uses. A translucent stair tower "knits" the two floors together and becomes a central visual element. Large sliding doors on the upper level open the interior to the exterior, thereby enhancing the connection of living spaces to the surrounding lake.
Photographs by Benjamin Benschneider

"A home's design should reflect the owner's dreams, yet it must also creatively synthesize the realities of program, budget and site."

—Bill Vandeventer

ABOVE & FACING PAGE: The Madison Park residence accommodates an active family of six while also serving as a platform for entertaining and displaying a growing collection of contemporary art. The clients emphasized that they wanted a house that would be family-oriented and functional—a house that performs—yet the design should also be architecturally challenging and provocative: a house that transforms the normative form of domestic architecture. The house's layout is developed in a three-dimensional composition that promotes the children's interaction with the art while maintaining separation from the errant soccer ball. Uses, organized vertically and horizontally about a light-filled gallery, are clearly identifiable through their architectural form, cladding and color.
Photographs by Benjamin Benschneider

"Natural light is always the fourth dimension in our work. It provides an undeniable sense of wellbeing that is critical to the experience of our homes."

—Tim Carlander

LEFT: Material selection and construction details in the Madison Park residence reinforce the project's conceptual design. Public-living functions are developed in a loft-like space on the main level. Private family functions on the upper floor are defined by an Alaskan yellow cedar skin. To the rear, service functions are clad in maintenance-free, Cor-Ten steel panels. The cantilevered office on the main level remains the special object; inserted into yet projecting from the main volume, it is clad inside and out with an ochre-colored cement stucco.

FACING PAGE: Seen from the entry hall and home office, a sculpture by Ann Gardner hangs at one end of the linear gallery. Lit from three sides, the sculpture's color and form complement the architecture.
Photographs by Benjamin Benschneider

"I've never been drawn to arbitrary complexity; as such, we believe our work should tend toward quiet, simple elegance over visual noise."

—Tim Carlander

ABOVE: The Sequim residence is a finely crafted wood structure rooted to a rustic masonry base. Cedar, stone and glass are the primary exterior materials; inside, the sole use of cedar and cherry as finish materials reflect an appreciation for the expressive character of wood. The home is set into a steeply sloping site; landscape retaining walls create multiple terraces at several levels. The diagonal slope of the site allows each terrace and deck to meet grade at various points around the house. Generally one room deep, the house is a simple form, stretching linearly across the width of the site. This allows for maximum views as well as natural light and cross ventilation in every space.

FACING PAGE: The C3 cabin was borne out of the desire to pare down and simplify, to escape from a world that has become more complex and demanding. Whereas the footprint may be small, this cabin lives large. With only 352 square feet on the main floor and 128 square feet up in the loft, it encompasses all the requirements of a home many times larger. Oversized glass doors provide abundant daylight and a sense of open space not typically found in a cabin this size. The home was designed with minimal maintenance in mind.
Photographs by Steve Keating Photography

BC Custom Homes, page 73

Bellan Construction, page 83

the structure

chapter two

Each custom home reflects a lifetime of observations and ideas of personal sanctuary. Depending on where future owners grew up, their cultural heritage and their exposure to world arts and architecture, the home they dream about typically incorporates elements of style and design innovations from different eras. In Oregon especially, custom homes also reflect demands for green products and sustainability. Bill Winkenbach has a decades-long history of interpreting such dreams, of adapting elements of style to create aesthetically pleasing yet truly comfortable homes. In 1991 he founded BC Custom Homes, which, in time, became widely recognized for its versatility and its portfolio of award-winning homes.

Bill discovered his passion for construction and his entrepreneurial spirit at an early age; he first picked up a hammer when he was sixteen. Today he is meticulous in his craft. Bill excels at the team approach, evident in his uncanny knack for putting together and guiding the right mix of talents and personalities that will best serve each individual client. With his rare combination of traits, Bill manages to raise the bar again and again for builders who strive to create works of art. Recently BC Custom Homes entered four homes in the prestigious Excellence Award competition for the greater Portland Metro area—and walked away with four First Place awards.

"Every home, in essence, is a melding of styles."

—Bill Winkenbach

BC Custom Homes

"We want to interpret the storybook lives of the owners."

—Bill Winkenbach

RIGHT & PREVIOUS PAGES: We wanted to take the idea of a storybook home and bring it to reality. Here, the fairytale aesthetic meets an Old World style. At the entrance, stone pillars support a radius arch, and within, a castle-style door and a gas lantern carry the mythical side of the home. For maximum integrity of our stucco system, we applied a rain screen, a redundant waterproof membrane, then applied a hand-troweled stucco faux-finish for an Old World look. The inside is designed to blend with the outdoors. The wall system allows the great room and family room to open up to 16 feet out to the covered porch; the huge fire pit and gas lamps make this space a great extension of the home and an entertaining spot for most of the year, and the stream just beyond carries a tranquil sound.
Photographs by Dwon Guvenir

"Think about where people gather—that's where the focus should be."

—Bill Winkenbach

ABOVE & RIGHT: Although the kitchen radiates elegance and grace, gourmet chefs know functionality when they see it. State-of-the-art, commercial-grade appliances are integrated with natural stone and environmentally friendly finishes. By focusing on function and livability, we created a kitchen and patio extension that is perfect for a family or large gatherings of friends.

FACING PAGE TOP: Repeating elements of style dominate the master bathroom. The graceful curve of the barrel-vault ceiling has repeats in the transom, in the arch above the shower and in the arch above the entrance to a walk-in closet.

FACING PAGE BOTTOM: A well-designed home has spaces that function as quiet retreats. The study's design elements and finishes issue a warm invitation to privacy.

Photographs by Dwon Guvenir

"Quality is absolutely essential—you have to have a keen eye for detail."

—Bill Winkenbach

ABOVE: We worked closely with the architect to realize the owner's dream of a French Country home. The entire exterior is clad in stone veneer. Wood-clad Marvin windows, unusual in the Pacific Northwest, reinforce the Old World character. A series of retaining walls allows the home to perch safely on a complex hillside and take advantage of commanding mountain views. Although the overall impression is one of being in the country, the home actually is close to downtown Portland.

FACING PAGE: Once inside, the interior finishes capture the full intent of the French Country estate. The winding staircase with travertine steps and unique wrought-iron rail, cast columns, Tuscan finish drywall and dark-stain hardwood millwork establishes the home as an architectural work of art.
Photographs by Jal Duncan

"Sustainability is a huge priority. It's an often-invisible yet dynamic factor in responsible building."

—Bill Winkenbach

ABOVE: The estate, in Pacific Northwest style, stretches 9,500 square feet around a central courtyard and magnificent swimming pool. Size aside, it incorporates green principles. All windows as well as the heating system have Energy-Star ratings. Its orientation maximizes passive solar heating to decrease the carbon footprint. The building strategy preserved the mature native trees at the site.

FACING PAGE: The custom home was built for a show. Once the owner saw the site, he said he wanted the home to look like something you would find in Colorado. We developed a floorplan, followed with elevation, until we had a great representative of that state's aesthetic. The master bath takes on a spacious approach; custom cabinetry enables the closet to be incorporated into the dressing area. With hidden washer and dryer, the spacious room has high utilitarian value. The kitchen of this home, with its stunning cabinetry, double island and the open connection to the nook and great room, is in keeping with our many award-winning homes. These few examples represent a microcosm of the scope of BC Custom Homes—we wanted to build with integrity through quality, and so we continue to strive for that principle.
Photographs by Dwon Guvenir

In the late '70s Michael Bellan learned the craft of fine homebuilding by working with his father on unique custom homes in the beautiful Santa Cruz Mountains in California. After moving to Seattle in 1979, he founded the company now known as Bellan Construction. As it grew from a one-man bag-carrying sole proprietorship to a team of like-minded, on-site project managers, site supervisors and highly skilled craftsman carpenters, the company has honed its communication and project management skills to blend with its remarkable technical expertise, allowing the company to participate fully in building some of the most remarkable architectural homes in the greater Seattle area.

The Bellan approach to construction is unique for a builder at this quality level. Rather than perform primarily as a company managing subcontractors, Michael Bellan offers his many years of experience and learning architecture, serving as an excellent resource for detailed collaboration with the clients and the architects. The firm is preferred by the finest architects in the area for projects that blend design development with the process of construction. The company philosophy is uniquely suited to this collaborative process due to the organization and management style of the team.

"The quality of the team members and their intimate understanding of fine architectural design is the preeminent advantage."

—Michael Bellan

BELLAN CONSTRUCTION

> "Projects that include architects and owners dedicated to excellence in building and design allow us to approach the process of building from the architectural viewpoint."
>
> —Michael Bellan

RIGHT & FACING PAGE: A very dark, badly remodeled house did not provide the new owners any feeling of home. The goal of the latest remodel was to provide a spatially unique, modern home in keeping with the 1950s' flavor while opening up all the rooms to each other. Designed by Robert Miller of the award-winning firm of Bohlin Cywinski Jackson and involving Amy Williams as project lead, this home won the coveted Honor Award at the 2008 Honor Awards for Washington Architecture through the Seattle Chapter of the AIA. The ipe-decked hallway figuratively divides the house in two, opening up the entertaining areas and the kitchen on one side and the bedrooms and baths on the other. You walk from the entry door down this hallway, and you come to another pivot door that swings open to allow you to walk outside. The architect's design offers windows where there might normally be walls, making rooms seem as though they are an extension of the outside. The design incorporates the use of architectural concrete with wood and steel—areas our firm has exceptional expertise in. As you wander the exterior grounds of the home, the concrete appears to be suspended in air in order to provide decks at different levels of the exterior. This was the perfect project for us to work closely with the architect and the homeowner during all of the construction process.
Photographs by Nic Lehoux Photography

PREVIOUS PAGES: The Queen Anne residence, designed by Suyama Peterson Deguchi, sits on the south slope of Queen Anne Hill and includes the extensive use of architectural concrete counterbalanced with wood and steel. The landscape softens the exacting architecture with beautiful water features and ipe wood screens and gates. This is a great piece of architecture that matched the owners' vision from the beginning.
Photographs by Robert Pisano, Robert Pisano Photography

"Using craftspeople with experience in all phases of construction, from concrete to the finest finish details, is essential to achieving the owners' goals and vision."

—Michael Bellan

ABOVE & FACING PAGE: The light-infused Medina residence sits lakeside on Lake Washington. The intent of this large-scale remodel and addition, designed by Brian Brand, a principal with Baylis Architects, was to provide a place for the homeowner's eclectic art collection while offering the opportunity to incorporate art into the actual design of the house. Additionally, the owner wanted a place where family and friends would feel welcome. This was accomplished by effectively dividing the casual and formal areas between two floors. We extensively collaborated with the owner to integrate several new art pieces into the home, such as handcarved dining-room doors, designed and crafted by local artisan Steve Jensen, and a beautiful glass wall, designed by Joe McDonnell, separating the hallway from the dining room using a steel framework incorporated with mahogany cabinetry by Bellan Shopworks. The design also included extensive use of architectural concrete counterbalanced with wood and steel. The lower floor is radiant-heated, tinted concrete while the majority of the exterior of the home is stucco along with metal used for the curved walls and staircases. The homeowner and our firm together crafted the beautiful master bathroom, which incorporates a custom-designed revolving mirror. The home functions as a showcase for art as well as a warm and inviting family home for children and friends.
Photographs by Ed Sozinho, Pro Image Photography

"The top priority is to craft architecture rather than to manage subcontractors."

—Michael Bellan

ABOVE & FACING PAGE: This home was also designed by Suyama Peterson Deguchi. Similar to other projects we have worked on, the homeowners were specifically looking for a design that would allow them to showcase their art in a home that was itself a piece of art. Granite wraps up the wall to form a simple fireplace surround. The kitchen is an ultramodern room with glossy white plastic laminate cabinets that actually look like lacquer. The floor is ash, but the countertops and the island are the same granite that is used elsewhere, achieving the homeowners' goal of minimal colors and materials. The exterior side of the house has an unobstructed view of Puget Sound. Floor-to-ceiling windows feature sliding doors that open onto a smooth-as-glass concrete terrace that runs the length of the house. A meandering gravel trail leads to an observation platform clinging to the side of this high-bank cliff.
Photographs courtesy of Bellan Construction

"The owners and architects' vision becomes a true reality through the performance of expert craftsmen and skilled management."

—Michael Bellan

ABOVE: The Madison Park home, designed by Eric Cobb of E. Cobb Architects, was a four-phase remodel. In each phase, the homeowner added more modern elements to what started out as an architecturally traditional residence and is now a beautiful blend of the traditional with the modern. The commercial-grade windows open onto a patio area that blends modernity while keeping the traditional feel of the original home.

FACING PAGE: Also designed by Eric Cobb, the Whidbey Island residence incorporates commercial-grade windows from ground to roof on the view side of the home. The remarkable stairs include architectural steel brackets, stringers and rails incorporated into a series of levels of open stair treads with no risers for maximum view. The exposed timber beams begin on the interior and extend across the entire width of the space to the exterior roofline and are then filled in with vertical grain fir.

Photographs by Paul Warchol, Warchol Photography

The natural environment in the northwest is rugged, grand and inspiring. Regional homes are conceived and built in relationship to the elements around them. They may be unadorned and modern, woven through with Japanese aesthetic and principles or infused with the local urban vernacular. As a builder, the process is made even more engaging by the use of native materials—huge boulders, slabs of wood, rusted steel—that are incorporated into many of the designs. In the northwest, nature is an influential member of the team, providing the set, setting and natural materials that help define this architecture.

The Seattle office of Dovetail General Contractors is a warm, lofty, industrial space enclosed by luminous colors and a garage door that slides up for immediate connection with the neighborhood outside. Open and simple, it reflects aspects that define the regional architectural style that the company specializes in building. Owner Adam Turner started out constructing fine furniture while still in high school and later applied his skills to well-designed homes. He has since brought together a talented and diverse group of builders, cabinetmakers and construction professionals, some of whom have design backgrounds. This group is an impressive and experienced assembly that embodies the company's commitment to high craft, communication and integrity.

"Building a person's home is layered and complex. There's a thrill about having mastery and control over so many moving parts and critical details."

—Adam Turner

DOVETAIL GENERAL CONTRACTORS

"Design and construction are challenging and exciting. Well supported by organization, communication and enthusiasm, the process can be extremely rewarding."

—Adam Turner

RIGHT: The project was an ongoing collaboration between homeowner, architect and builder. The owner is a graphic designer who hired the original architect of record to help him redesign the house. Poorly constructed by the first builder 40 years prior, the home was dark and heavy; we updated it by fully opening the south wall with glazing, removing two massive concrete Trombe walls and installing steel drag struts in their place. The result is a home full of bright, open and engaging spaces. Architecture by Mark Millett.

PREVIOUS PAGES: The house was designed to be warm, comfortable, modern and low maintenance. The selected siding is traditional face-sealed stucco, and we hung it on a rain-screen system. While this approach minimizes moisture entrapment, it also complicates detailing around all openings and transitions, sometimes in surprising ways. Resolving those types of complications is a lot of what makes building houses so engaging. Architecture by John Fleming.
Photographs by Benjamin Benschneider

"Building is in part an exercise in communication. Concentrating on clear communication is the best way to ensure that the project is a positive experience for everyone."

—Adam Turner

ABOVE: On all projects, we source materials that are durable and budget-minded and that fit with the aesthetic of the design. The house is sided in clear western red cedar and cement board, a perfect mix of a locally derived natural material combined with a budget-conscious, manufactured product. Architecture by DeForest Architects and B+O Habitats.

FACING PAGE: We worked closely with the architects to create a space that is both voluminous and intimate. With precisely matched grain and reveals, 11-foot-high cabinets wrap from the kitchen, down the stairs and into the hall on the floor below. A cantilevered steel balcony connects the upper levels with the great room, office and bedroom levels. Architecture by DeForest Architects and B+O Habitats.

Photographs by Benjamin Benschneider

"All sizable construction projects involve tough decisions concerning budget, design and scheduling. Through honest and open communication, these decisions can become a source of gratification."

—Adam Turner

ABOVE: A single steel column supports the massive moment connection that provides structure for the floor above. The kitchen pivots off that column. It is wide and airy, providing space and light, which works well with the heavy steel beams that intersect the ceiling. Architecture by Leah Martin, Verge AD.
Photograph by Leah Martin

FACING PAGE TOP: Our ability to work well as a team gives us control over the challenges of evolving design. The condominium is in a post-tension slab building and required that we fabricate to the most precise tolerances. We worked very closely with the owner to understand exactly how she wanted to live in the small space. Each piece of the design was prototypical, made to her specifications. Architecture by Josh Brevort. Interior design by Steven Hensel.
Photograph by Benjamin Benschneider

FACING PAGE BOTTOM: The big idea in the project is the way the cabinetry defines the entire living space. We built an L-shaped core of casework: The north side serves as the bedroom closet, laundry and bath; the west side creates the entry hall and storage; the east end is the owner's office; and the south side becomes this kitchen. There are no doors in the condominium, yet the spaces feel surprisingly private. Architecture by Josh Brevort. Interior design by Steven Hensel.
Photograph by Benjamin Benschneider

"We like building creative, challenging and engaging things. The scale is less important than how interesting the project is."

—Adam Turner

RIGHT: One of our most interesting projects, the tower serves as a model for a future residence to be constructed on the exact location. The three levels of the tower are at the precise levels of the future house, allowing the owner and architect to understand the home's relationship to the landscape. The curved roof, V-brackets and shield are all representative of the architectural details that will define the residence. All timber for the structure was cut and milled on site from the forest path that the tower overlooks. Architecture by Robert Edson Swain.
Photograph by Adam Turner

FACING PAGE TOP: Nestled between a cottage and a bungalow, the house was a modern interpretation of a traditional form. The young owner wanted the custom home to meet contemporary needs while holding a certain nostalgia for the old farmhouse aesthetic. Incorporating details from both worlds ensured the project's success. Architecture by Frank Dill.
Photograph by Benjamin Benschneider

FACING PAGE BOTTOM: The kitchen exemplifies the melding of the two distinct architectural forms: the modern and the traditional. Open shelves and a big old-fashioned farm sink rest inside face frame cabinetry without protruding hardware, making the kitchen an exemplary melding of modern and traditional styles. Architecture by Frank Dill.
Photograph by Benjamin Benschneider

People build on the West Coast for the remarkable views. However, one of the downfalls is that some of the best sites are steeply sloped. This results in a different kind of build—sensitivity must be applied in the planning stages to avoid slide, drainage and other seismic issues. Mother Nature has given a challenge, and EH Construction steps out to reveal quality homes that have demanded specialized construction techniques, not for the faint of heart.

Lyell Ernst and Brent Heath have known each other for some 50 years. As young men, they worked for Lyell's father, a contractor who imparted inspiration and construction philosophies to the boys. For the last 25 years, the two have worked together as EH Construction, forming homes that reflect the owners as well as the architects, turning, as they say, dreams into reality. Coming up with ways to manipulate a home to conform to its landscape is part of the fun, but realizing that a vision has manifested as a result of good building is truly rewarding.

"The crux of the process is matchmaking: Owners and architects should fall in love with the home."

—Lyell Ernst

EH CONSTRUCTION

RIGHT: The owners of the Seattle home wanted a very open feel by bringing the outside in. To get the open air feeling, we developed a metal sliding system, forming a virtual moving wall so that outdoors and indoors fuse. Keeping to wood and steel, the materials are simplified to the core.

PREVIOUS PAGES: The design for the home called for something contemporary that would use lots of steel. To accent the industrial look, we used slabs of concrete, corrugated steel siding and wood—VG fir. The resulting structure is sharp and modern, a great transition from the natural surroundings.

Photographs by Benjamin Benschneider

"Traditional or contemporary, large or small, a dream home becomes reality through applied experience."

—Brent Heath

ABOVE: Steel can be so antique looking. We found this old water pipe lying around on the site and incorporated it into the design as a water feature. We're always looking for unique finishes.

FACING PAGE: Taking advantage of tremendous views, we employed a catwalk that, like the porch, allowed the steel to rust. Rust has a way of instantly aging a home, and for a rainy area, the aged aesthetic works perfectly here.
Photographs by Cheryl James

ABOVE: Because of the sensitive site area, we constructed a 12-inch-thick, concrete retaining wall. Rocks were craned in to keep with a natural feeling. Floor-to-ceiling doors open the formal dining out to the courtyard. The site is about 20 feet below street level, so as you continually move downward, steel stairs line your route.

FACING PAGE TOP: If you want views here, you get slopes. This is not only a test in the design stages but also in construction—bringing materials in and, of course, giving careful consideration to the neighbors.

FACING PAGE BOTTOM: The homeowner spends a lot of time in China and Taiwan, and the granite bowl made the trip back, ending in the guest powder room. It was paired with a grooved, leather-like tile and a metal fabricated countertop. Coming down the staircase you are greeted by a massive stone, entering through the sliding doors into the kitchen. The blackened steel was designed to fit the color scheme.

Photographs by Eduardo Calderón

"Quality and diversity: You bring the former, the latter always follows."

—Brent Heath

ABOVE LEFT: Cedar siding runs throughout, melding the home into its surroundings. Looking up to the home, you can see the challenges of a hillside build. Smooth transitions are required, and, working with the owner and architect, we were able to maximize motion.

ABOVE RIGHT: The motif called for horizontal lines, from the shell down to the tile in the powder room. We crafted the siding with cedar, and coming down into the home gives a distinct layering, as though you are descending through geological strata.

FACING PAGE: In all, the home is a prime example of hillside structuring. Blending natural elements, such as the boulders, with solid material—wood and steel—we crafted a home that is aesthetically unique with the strength of the hills themselves.

Photographs by Eduardo Calderón

There is a long line of Kesslers that can stretch back prior to WWII with Homer Kessler. Homer Kay Kessler— Kurt's father—came back from the Battle of the Bulge and saw a gap in the ability to construct homes. The people in Brookings had limited access to nails, glass, paint and other requisite supplies, so the Kesslers decided that they would fill the void, one element at a time. Homer Kay Kessler made his name in construction in the early 1960s, developing a cabinet shop and building homes. The Kessler path of reinvigorating the Pacific Northwest with remarkable homes had been set by the time Kurt Kessler was 13, when he came into the business. When Kurt turned 24, he put some tools into his truck and headed out to Bend, Oregon, to develop Kurt Kessler Kustom Builder.

Kurt built 30 homes in four years before life in Brookings was calling him back. He moved back and pushed through the recession of the early '80s by doing odd jobs. Kurt soon reinvigorated his company with the sole purpose of developing high-end homes that truly speak to quality, the old German quality of fit-and-finish building. Kurt wanted precision in the craft, and by customizing each project and melding each with years of experience, he has reached a good place. But lately Lance Kessler, the fourth generation, has also joined ranks, putting a 21st-century spin on the business. And from here, the business can build.

"Beach cottage, Mediterranean estate, contemporary dwelling or log cabin, the home has to be a reflection of its inhabitants."

—Kurt Kessler

KURT KESSLER KUSTOM BUILDER INC.

"Your reputation comes from the work. So the work has to be perfect."

—Kurt Kessler

RIGHT: Oceanfront communities are a great place to blend homes with the environment. Here, in Brookings, Oregon, Harris Beach Estates pushes up to Harris Beach State Park with sloped lots viewing the ocean and plenty of earth tones—the estates exemplify a Frank Lloyd Wright theme.

PREVIOUS PAGES LEFT: Handmade columns line the entry with a mosaic tile floor and kitchen walls of Rocky Mountain quartzite. A limited land footprint can still hold a high-quality beachfront home.

PREVIOUS PAGES RIGHT: The beach at the north jetty side of Port of Brookings Harbor on the southern Oregon coast is amazing. We took the retaining wall to the beach with the vegetation line set back. Again, Rocky Mountain quartzite makes an appearance.
Photographs by William Ferry

"Pride of ownership comes out of the strife for perfection."

—Kurt Kessler

ABOVE: The ocean was our inspiration. We left room for a great, ocean-vista sculpture with white oak over granite countertops. Imaginative cabinetry meets tasteful quality.

FACING PAGE TOP: The oceanfront home has nice style and is designed to take advantage of the view. The beautiful location, with beach access, has a small building site and sits at the edge of the bluff, for which we utilized large and deep concrete piers for the foundation. The home really blends with the location, bringing the wow factor.

FACING PAGE BOTTOM: We opened up the master bath, bringing in lots of lights in the shower. We worked with many craftsmen in a limited space to capture these dream bath features.

Photographs by William Ferry

"It's a gratifying experience to produce quality homes."

—Kurt Kessler

ABOVE LEFT: This is an entryway that you won't forget. We blended wood with stone to capture the theme of the Pacific Ocean just outside.

ABOVE RIGHT: The entryway shows some of our versatility. Old World red oak styles with the solid look of stone. You'll wonder, "Is this real?"

FACING PAGE: At ocean hillsides, geology must be closely considered. A beautiful split entry features blended wood, stone and style on the Frank Lloyd Wright-themed home.
Photographs by William Ferry

"My final walkthrough is the confirmation of the owner's dream."

—Kurt Kessler

ABOVE LEFT: An open kitchen with a recessed ceiling has lots of light to work with. The custom cabinets were made in our shop as always. We worked painstakingly to capture the owners' desires so that the custom home keeps up with the ocean views, which are to die for.

ABOVE RIGHT: We special ordered the Brazilian cork bark wall paneling to bring some interest into the bathroom for an exotic look.

FACING PAGE: The custom log home is a blending of logs and modern products. Big rooms with big views, big lights and big beauty, the log home exudes the woodsy, Pacific Northwest style.
Photographs by William Ferry

At the end of Homer's epic, Odysseus' true identity is revealed through the quality craftwork of his bed. One could argue, then, that a true odyssey can only be accomplished with fine craftsmanship. Odyssey Builders was developed with the idea of high ethical standards being applied to every element of the unique projects the firm takes on. Bringing many disparate elements to form a unified whole is the goal of each build so that whether the project be a new home or a remodel, the end product is greater than the parts. The homes that Odyssey Builders takes on are innovative and thoughtful in construction as well as in execution.

Founded in 1981 by David Crocker, Odyssey Builders is always on the lookout for interesting projects. All long-term employees, the core group of people on staff brings in a range of different abilities to form a very collaborative effort. The team's commitment is to build homes that are good for the owners, that reduce environmental impact and that have exceptional, sustainable value. Though Dave has moved his role to an advisory position while Matt Cantrell and Michele McCartney have stepped in, Odyssey Builders still maintains the principle elements of Dave's original idea: to build with innovation.

"A little bit of invention is essential."

—Matt Cantrell

ODYSSEY BUILDERS

"Very singular designs for each individual come out of careful thought, which doesn't cost much."

—Matt Cantrell

ABOVE: Elements of universal design can be seen throughout the home. We were brought in very early while the owner—a quadriplegic—and the architect were still working on the design. Freedom of moment was required throughout, such as in the shower, which we waterproofed in its entirety. We also built a little nook into the wall for a wheel chair.

FACING & PREVIOUS PAGES: The design had elements that crossed somewhere between a warehouse and a Japanese temple. Exposed structures exist throughout. The plywood panels work great because they are not only aesthetically fascinating, but they are also easily replaced. Thematically, we combined steel and wood—steel trim and railing consistently crosses with birchwood and Douglas fir. Aesthetically, the frosted-glass sliding doors offset the veritable block of wood that houses the discreet Murphy bed. Built specifically with the homeowner in mind, the home required a level of high innovation, which is where our hearts lie. Architecture by DeForest Architects. *Photographs by Benjamin Benschneider*

"Constant education in the field creates crucial variety among the homes."

—Matt Cantrell

RIGHT: The 1950s' house, originally designed by Paul Kirk, had great architectural interest. The homeowner understood that a combination of the old and the new would preserve the interest. The great thing about coming into a project early on is that, as builders, we bring heavy experience for what works and what does not. Here is where you get a little bit of invention. For example, the milestone floor: A thin veneer of fine, cement-based plaster is very smooth, has a lot of depth and is waterproof though it is made to look like dark concrete. Architecture by Bjarko Serra Architects.
Photograph by Benjamin Benschneider

"Different abilities at work make for exciting, diverse solutions."

—Matt Cantrell

ABOVE: Remodels have a level of precision that must be extraordinarily high. Here, the collective experience of the workers can be seen in many rooms. In the bathroom, there is a coordination of trades—tiler, carpenter, plumber—each having to perfectly align cabinets with windows that already existed, a full tile layout with existing structural elements and plumbing with cabinetry that does not go to the floor.

FACING PAGE: One of the big issues with remodels is the house settling. You get what you get, more or less—homes settle, get out of line, and you have to build around that. Contemporary architecture performs very well when you get those alignments to work.
Photographs by Benjamin Benschneider

"Simply put, we want to build cool houses."
—Matt Cantrell

ABOVE & FACING PAGE: Many trades worked in tandem on the second floor of the 1950s' house. Just beyond the front door, a steel column existed. We had to build around that with a hutch of sorts, with glass, wood, steel and electrical workers each taking part in the piece. Tied in with the laminated Douglas fir floor, the black cabinetry lends itself to opening the space up, proving a remarkable solution to a problem that required innovation.
Photographs by Benjamin Benschneider

Casa bella Oregon, page 135   Michael Homchick Stoneworks Inc., page 145

elements of structure

chapter three

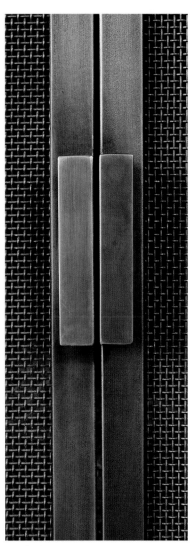

Steve Lopes Blacksmith, page 161

Walter Gordinier Studios, LLC, page 193

Metal Solutions, page 175

CASA BELLA OREGON

Portland, Oregon

"The beauty of stone is that you are always looking at something different."

—MJ Hajari

ABOVE & FACING PAGE: Collaborating with conscientious stone inspectors from California to Brazil and as far away as China, we have a wonderful selection of natural stone. It's a joy to invite design professionals and their clients to explore our offerings in the warehouse and put together plans in the designer room as we crane lift large slabs over to the viewing window for inspection. Cabinetry, countertop and backsplash options rotate independently on two carousels so that it's easy to visualize what the stone will look like in place. This powerful conceptual tool is a Casa bella exclusive that makes the creative process smooth, pleasant and rewarding.
Photographs by Fabienne Photography & Design

"You must have a vision of what to do with stone. That's where you find individuality."

—MJ Hajari

RIGHT: Our grand staircase uses three-centimeter Peruvian travertine slab for the treads, hand rails and side kick plates. The truly exquisite risers are perfectly bookmatched onyx slab panels backlit by LEDs to highlight the translucent nature of the material. A premade mosaic medallion finishes off the landing. To the right of the staircase, the tub deck is clad in rare Breccia Oniciata marble. This is really a chance to explore stone possibilities.
Photograph by Fabienne Photography & Design

"Stone use is great for form, giving a strong Old World feel."

—MJ Hajari

ABOVE LEFT: A fully functioning kitchen greets visitors to our showroom. The Pompeii Exotica granite slab counters demonstrate five popular edge options: ogee, waterfall, flat polished, 3/8-inch round and chiseled edge. Water jet inlays grace the countertop and full-height backsplash behind the range, and the coordinating cabinets are European Stemmed Beech with a custom stain. Fabricated and installed by American Marble & Granite, Camas, Washington.

ABOVE RIGHT: The elegant fireplace in our reception area is an example of the kind of fine workmanship possible in natural stone. The Forest Bordeaux granite featured on the hearth and the arch on the surround are hand-shaped and polished to achieve the desired curves. The radial hearth base of Metallic granite is likewise ground and polished by hand. This unique stone is also featured on the surround and mantel. Fabricated and installed by Stone Center, Portland, Oregon.

FACING PAGE: Simms Fine Homes, one of Lake Oswego's foremost homebuilders, uses full slab on the entry floor to create an outstanding showpiece. The design, precision-cut using high-tech water jet equipment, features Golden Musk, Bordeaux Terracotta, Black Beauty and Copper Canyon granites.
Photographs by Fabienne Photography & Design

"When multiple, artisanal products come together aesthetically, you know you are at the high end."

—MJ Hajari

LEFT: The walls of the showroom entry are clad in bookmatched Rainforest Green slab. This warm-toned marble is the perfect counterpart to a one-of-a-kind brass soaking tub.

FACING PAGE TOP LEFT: A unique copper trough sink is set into a vanity of Velvet Taupe marble featuring a chiseled edge and an antiqued finish.

FACING PAGE TOP RIGHT: The carved natural stone sink is just one of the many pieces of functional art to be found at Casa bella.

FACING PAGE BOTTOM LEFT: A flared vessel sink sits atop an Andino Dark travertine vanity in our showroom. A mosaic border and two sizes of rope liner complete the grouping.

FACING PAGE BOTTOM RIGHT: Polished, vein-cut travertine tiles are punctuated by a stone-and-glass mosaic border and travertine chair rail in the classic bath.
Photographs by Fabienne Photography & Design

"There isn't anything you can't do with stone."

—MJ Hajari

LEFT: Peruvian travertine pavers are laid in a Versailles pattern on the pool and hot tub deck by Brentwood Homes. The travertine's earthy colors and rustic finish are complemented by the home's beautiful natural setting. Give the quality that the project needs, and everything turns out beautifully.
Photograph by Fabienne Photography & Design

MICHAEL HOMCHICK STONEWORKS INC.

Kenmore, Washington

"Stone fabrication, a subtractive process, is the inverse of most other art forms. You only remove what you don't want."

—Michael Homchick

ABOVE & FACING PAGE: The original fireplace was low and squatty, an eyesore in the room. We tore out the old firebox, damper and smoke chamber and put the plan together for this fireplace. Building piece by piece, we used computer-controlled, three-dimensional renderings while handcarving the detailing. Stone quality is, of course, essential; we look all over the world for quarries, hand-selecting our material. At its completion, the work is earthquake-safe and is a great statement of solidness.
Photographs by Bryce Mohan

"There is a stately longevity in stonework—a federal-building aesthetic."

—Michael Homchick

ABOVE & FACING PAGE: A Mercer Island client wanted to show a dichotomy of wood and stone, getting rid of the floor-to-ceiling brick fireplace that existed. Using Texas limestone that is consistent in texture, we crafted a very regal fireplace with a classical theme. Tiffany Widdifield, our sculptor, handcarved an acanthus-scroll pattern on the corbels. This was free-form work—no machines were used.
Photographs by Bryce Mohan

"With stone, you know you're making future antiques. They last forever."

—Michael Homchick

ABOVE: We have a library of classical architecture, and so when homeowners want a colorful, rustic alternative, we hit the books. Taking from the old Greek and Roman ideas of patterns, mosaics are a great chance to think of stonework at its smallest scale. The stones are not artificially colored; there are 30 different stones from all over the world in this mosaic. Using a wide range of quarries means that we can blend plenty of natural colors for realization.

FACING PAGE: This new, French-style home required an array of period stones. The vanity was fabricated using Calacatta Oro from Italy. The result gives a 17th-century feel on first approach, but the edge cut has an interesting, modern quality to it. We've built our reputation on authentic pieces, and having many craftsmen on staff, we're able to unify our individual strengths.
Photographs by Bryce Mohan

"High-quality stone surfaces are like jewelry for your home."

—Michael Homchick

ABOVE: The galley of a 112-foot yacht is the ultimate as far as quality goes. Installing stone in a boat requires special expertise. Because boats flex in rough water, we used epoxy-impregnated carbon fiber fused to stone that is less than one-fourth of an inch thick to allow for flexibility. The exposed edges are built up, giving the illusion of thickness.

FACING PAGE TOP: Rosso Damasco marble runs across the countertop and up the backsplash. By circling the globe in search of the best of exotic stones, we are able to provide designers with a palette of color and texture. Handcrafted stone is one of those things that never goes out of style.

FACING PAGE BOTTOM: We handcarve custom sinks out of block. The white sink was carved to precisely match the existing built-in furniture. Marble sinks often have Italian themes, such as this grape design, carved by my daughter. Due to the hours required to sculpt stone, carved pieces forever maintain their value. Well-crafted stonework is inherently heirloom quality.
Photographs by Bryce Mohan

"For a refined and delicate touch, nothing surpasses stone."

—Claudio Gonda

ABOVE & FACING PAGE: As an importer of natural stone, we see limestone in all its variations. It can appear in spaces that seek a cool stone that is long-lasting, as in the fireplace, which features Villefort Ramage limestone, as well as the bathroom's limestone wainscoting that borders Italian travertine. The occasional appearance of fossilized sea animals is also a great bonus.

Photographs by Lautaro Gabriel Gonda

"The grandeur of the Old World is inherent in stone."

—Claudio Gonda

LEFT: Variations of tile uses can be seen in the Calacatta marble bathroom—a great alternative to traditional forms.

FACING PAGE: The bathroom uses Brazilian multicolored slate along with limestone to find harmony through differing materials.
Photographs by Lautaro Gabriel Gonda

"Bringing stone into the home pulls nature right into the heart of life."
—Claudio Gonda

ABOVE & FACING PAGE: Fireplaces are a great opportunity to utilize uncommon materials, such as soapstone slab, which, when engraved, offers a mysterious elegance unlike most materials.
Photographs by Lautaro Gabriel Gonda

"The world is full of stone, and we cross the whole to find it."

—Claudio Gonda

ABOVE: The kitchen features Verde Pradera granite slab, whose cool colors counteract the darkness of the room.

FACING PAGE TOP: In another kitchen, Labradorite blue granite is the perfect complement to dark woods.

FACING PAGE BOTTOM: Used for centuries in carvings, the supple nature of soapstone allows strength and pliability for differing designs.
Photographs by Lautaro Gabriel Gonda

Port Townsend, Washington

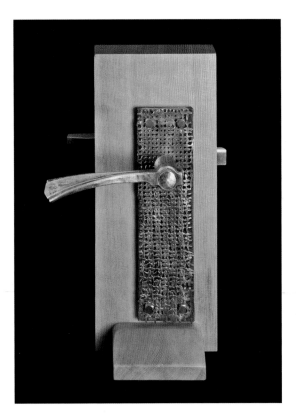 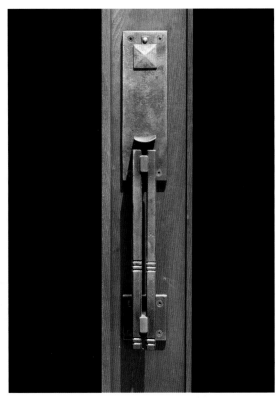

"Metalwork detailing is like good jazz: What makes the solo really good is to have a solid rhythm section."

—Steve Lopes

ABOVE LEFT: The majority of my work is decorative architectural metalwork with a sculptural flavor. Door hardware is a great place to explore something different. The home had an Asian feel to it, with shoji screens and even granite that was pulled from a highway on the Yangtze River. To give a worn-out feeling, I hammered two layers of mesh to create the textured backplate. As an accent, the bronze lever is rotated into a soft curve.
Photograph by Craig Wester

ABOVE RIGHT: Crafting a door piece that is clean and angular, very contemporary, offers something different from the mesh piece. Blacksmithing for architecture is an interview process, and when you can pull out the design from the homeowner, you find the path. It's a people-reading kind of job.
Photograph by Steve Lopes

FACING PAGE: The idea was to create a structural interplay between the timber-frame trusses and the chandelier. Exposed bolts, outriggers and bars—these are the elements that really make a showpiece fit right in with the rest of the room.
Photograph by Art Grice

RIGHT: The whole house was designed around the central wall-hanging, created in D'aubusson, France, by the Maison de Gobelin tapestry makers in the late 17th century. The railing needed to be simple and rhythmic without competing with the tapestry. The pickets—which bring that rhythm—overlap like gothic arches but in a more organic fashion. While the stems are six inches apart, the petals open up, giving solidity to the movement downstairs. Tied in with the airy light fixture, the sculptural essence of the metalwork has a Craftsman, slightly Asian feel—a nice complement to the tapestry.

Photograph by Roger Turk, Northlight Photography

"Like a book, blacksmithing shows its method, the work that the steel has been through. Forged metal is always a good read."

—Steve Lopes

ABOVE: The railing panel has a classic artisan feel to it. The railing piece uses 96 feet of steel in a three-foot-square segment. The adjacent wine-cellar gate, however, begged for something different. To avoid grape clichés, I took the home's proximity to water as a theme, creating a rippling, reflecting pattern that alludes to nothing in particular, but that gives both a feel of water and a suggestion of pruned vines. A little bit of thought goes a long way.

FACING PAGE: Steel reacts really well with large beams and stone. Coming into a contemporary home, a clean and simple place, the pendant lamps and wall sconces offer a strong Asian feel to the lodge. The mica shades are perfect with the copper banding. These are hand-hammered, hand-formed designs that really push for distinction.
Photographs by Craig Wester

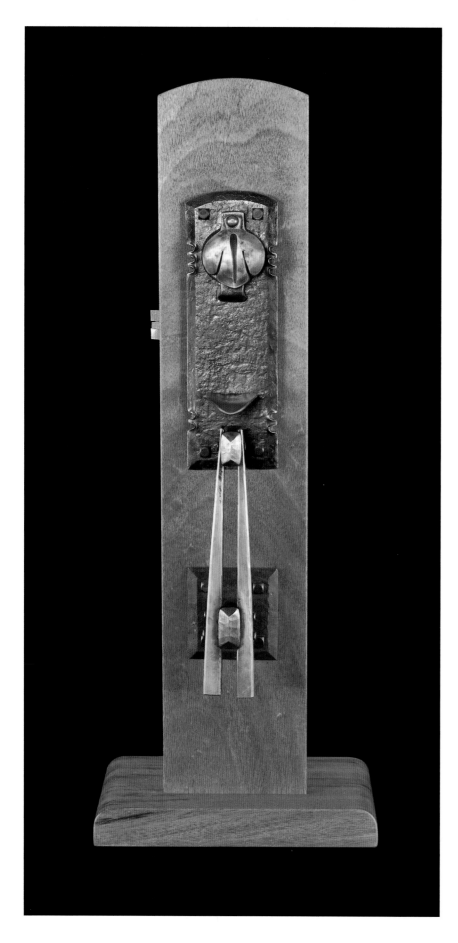

"Trial and evolution form the core of this kind of work. You heat and hammer, forging the iron until something fantastic appears."

—Steve Lopes

LEFT: Door hardware can be very interesting. He may want a big, sturdy grip while she wants a thin, airy handle. Split bronze pieces achieved the same width without the heaviness—suggesting mass without being massive. The typical lamb's tongue latch is visually solid, but light can come through those split pieces. The leaf-shaped lock cover augments the texture-art backplate. The whole is a great blend of aesthetics.
Photograph by Craig Wester

FACING PAGE: Because of the sheer volume of the fireplace, the chandelier needed to be big. I had this idea of a child's toy dangling above the space. There are eight planes: Four are white and horizontal while the other four are amber, tapered to a 45-degree angle. Since it is pretty much the only light in the room, the lighting had to function on multiple levels. Down-lighting can be switched to indirect lighting that is seen through the planes, up to the ceiling. The dining room light and railing are great Craftsman pieces that really harmonize with the chandelier. Melding these sculptural metals with architecture is really what modern blacksmithing is about.
Photograph by Vance Fox Photography

MARK NEWMAN DESIGN IN WOOD

"When it comes to style, I am a committed chameleon ... beauty as well as good design come in many styles."

—Mark Newman

ABOVE: My definition of architectural woodworking is very simple: It means attached to the building. The Jeff Lamb-designed, jatobá bedroom pieces—bed, bureau and fireplace—are attached to the building and beautifully woven into the home's architecture.
Photographs by Richard H. Strode

FACING PAGE: The historic house needed an addition to allow for outdoor entertaining or even calm moments of solitude by the double fireplace. We did all of the exterior woodwork—windows, pilasters, balustrade, columns, frieze and crown. The details are similar to the original, demonstrating the value of working in many different styles.
Photograph by Rick Charlton

"An artist is motivated by a vision; a craftsman by the love of style, process or materials; a designer by solving problems. When all three of these creative motivations work together, really great work happens."

—Mark Newman

ABOVE LEFT: The Jeff Lamb design, again made of jatobá, cantilevers over the table to define the dining room in an otherwise open great room.

ABOVE RIGHT & FACING PAGE: Wood was the driving force behind this project, requiring a very tight working relationship among the homeowner, the designer and me. Throughout the home, the African woods sapele and wenge show up thematically, as in the art gallery hallway. In both the master bedroom and master bathroom, the theme continues, showing very careful arrangements that work in harmony with the architecture.
Photographs by Richard H. Strode

"You have to love what you do. That is the motivation."

—Mark Newman

ABOVE: The stair rail was the most difficult bend we ever performed because of the sheer tightness of the turn. We had to build a structure to hold the rail in place. Once you put glue on the wood, you have about 10 minutes to set the rail. We spent an entire day practicing for the 10 minutes just to figure out the exact sequence since there would be no turning back. The result was clearly worth the effort.
Photographs by Rick Charlton

FACING PAGE: Within the context of its environment, an architectural piece may have many functions. The piece may show its function, as with this dining-room display shelf, or it may hide its function, as with the hidden coat closet. On the latter, a cabinet pivots to reveal a secret doorway to a small storage space. This is the job of a designer, to conceive and to realize.
Top photograph by Richard H. Strode
Bottom photograph by Joel Newman

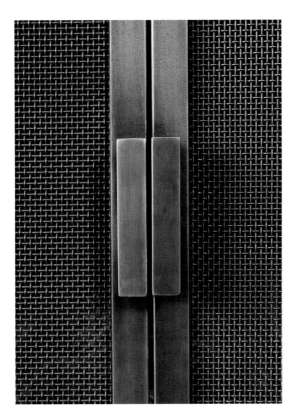 

"I try to take a comprehensive approach to design. I want the inside of the fireplace door to have the same level of finish and aesthetic as the outside."

—Steven Northey

ABOVE: Cabinet-style doors open to the firebox and are made of industrial mesh and structural steel; we accented the contemporary design with forged handles. The blackened, pitted and hand-waxed finish creates a rich and natural-looking patina.

FACING PAGE: We clad the original masonry fireplace of the mid-century residence in reclaimed scrap and structural steel. The hearth, surround and doors have been darkened and waxed. The use of recycled materials and traditional hand-applied finishes helps reduce the impact of the work on the environment.
Photographs by Dave Schiefelbein

"Creating architectural pieces in metal takes careful planning, yet we must allow the design to evolve and reveal itself."

—Steven Northey

ABOVE: A detail of the railing rivets echoes the precise, geometric design of the steel balustrade. We etched the surface of the metal to expose the crystalline structure of the steel.

FACING PAGE: The Craftsman-style railing is a fine counterpoint to the warm organic tones of the surrounding wood panels.
Photographs by Dave Schiefelbein

"It is important to consider each component and how it coexists in its environment. The relationship of the materials to the site is paramount."

—Steven Northey

ABOVE: Mounted to follow the fluid architecture of the home's curvilinear balcony, the custom fabricated bronze oval railcap has a deep, antiqued finish.
Photograph by Dave Schiefelbein

FACING PAGE TOP LEFT: The custom cast bronze volute and railcap exhibits a rich, patinated luster; we added a bronze wrap to highlight the forged steel handrail bracket.
Photograph by Steven Northey

FACING PAGE TOP RIGHT: From the Japanese term *yareigeta*, or "broken grid," the stair guardrail's design is based on an abstraction of kanji script.
Photograph by Steven Northey

FACING PAGE BOTTOM LEFT: The hand-forged guardrail is reminiscent of wild grasses.
Photograph by Dave Schiefelbein

FACING PAGE BOTTOM RIGHT: Blackened and waxed undulating ribbons of steel transform into artful balusters while the solid newel post mimics split and hewn timbers throughout the home.
Photograph by Steven Northey

OLD WORLD DOOR

Seattle, Washington

"The entry door should speak to the overall character of a home and anticipate its interior design. It is the focal point of the home."

—John Gardner

ABOVE: This walnut entry door opens to a small hotel in Paso Robles. The rustic hand-distressed wood is a perfect fit for a wine country inn in California.
Photograph by John Gardner

FACING PAGE: The arched entry of this unique home is framed by cement blocks set in a round turret below three square windows. It stands as well between an elliptical arched window on the left and a more traditional square window on the right. Our iron and glass door provided just the right blend of shape, pattern and texture to capture the eclectic theme of this home.
Photograph by Steve Gardner

"The best results are achieved when you think of it not as a door, but as vertical furniture."

—Steve Starwalt

ABOVE: Facing a small Florida lake, the terrace on this home is shaded by a louvered arbor that extends to the pool, which is enclosed by a dramatic wall of louvered doors and shutters. The absolute size—both in width and height—of this door system is an impressive sight from any vantage. The traditional plantation doors and shutters were manufactured in cypress and use the three-inch-wide louvers of the old Florida style while the bright, stainless-steel hinges and locksets add an appropriate nautical feel for a home surrounded by water on both sides. The balcony wall showcases another series of Old World Door shutters that add significantly to the home's overall appeal.
Photograph by Everett & Soule

FACING PAGE TOP: An iron gate leads into the courtyard of this Spanish-style ranch home in Santa Barbara, California. To round out the western theme, Old World Door also provided the shutters and iron crosses on the windows. It's truly all about the details!
Photograph by Steve Gardner

FACING PAGE BOTTOM LEFT: Beveled-diamond glass pieces are embedded with leaded glass, illustrating the variety of possibilities when you use your imagination.
Photograph by Scott Lance

FACING PAGE BOTTOM RIGHT: The plank-style entry door with a rustic grill over the speakeasy is surely the centerpiece of this magnificent entry.
Photograph by Lance Waite

"These gateways frame the ideal picture, to your home and to your life."

—Steve Gardner

ABOVE: The owner of Hotel Cheval carried with her an image of an antique door that she wanted replicated for the entrance to her hotel's lobby bar. From the center-mount doorknob to the antique mail slot and custom speakeasy, Old World Door helped her bring this vision to life.
Photograph by John Gardner

FACING PAGE TOP LEFT: The wall of panels creates interest and the mystery of perhaps a secret door.
Photograph by Scott Lance

FACING PAGE TOP RIGHT: Using the design of John Delibos, principal of Concepts In Design, Las Vegas, Old World Door built this architecturally complex entry of stained glass—on swinging panels—mounted on an iron door and set below opposing concave and convex lines in the transom.
Photograph by John Gardner

FACING PAGE BOTTOM LEFT: No matter what style, it's the details that add warmth and character to a home. Our iron shop crafts these elements, such as the cross iron piece above the entry.
Photograph by Scott Lance

FACING PAGE BOTTOM RIGHT: Gateways, like doorways, can frame a beautiful picture. While the fountain is the focal point here, the iron gate sets the stage by adding an Old World feel to the courtyard.
Photograph by Steve Gardner

RICHARD LANDON DESIGN

Bellevue, Washington

"A well-designed home has a certain musicality to it. As I design, I'm composing with shape, color and texture, as if with notes, rhythms and harmonies."

—Richard Landon

ABOVE: We designed this kitchen as a collection of furniture pieces, such as the built-in, sub-zero refrigerator resembling an armoire. Subtle details create interest throughout—each cabinetry section is a unique design. Three well-placed sinks make the elegant kitchen highly functional as well.
Photograph by Jonathan Edwards

FACING PAGE: Restructuring the kitchen's outside wall to increase the window's height now allows the tall homeowner to actually see the sky! In order not to have as many wall cabinets, the base ones are both deeper and taller, creating significantly more storage and usable counters. Visually, the kitchen emphasizes the horizontal by having the center drawer taller than the bottom. Orbital-finished stainless-steel countertops, zebra wood cabinets, glass and aluminum all give the kitchen a distinctly masculine feel, balanced with the femininity of the island's "stiletto heel" legs.
Photograph by Roger Turk

"We all have memories of places that have drawn us to them, inspired us or given us refuge and, in turn, powerfully affect what feels right to us."

—Richard Landon

ABOVE: A steel-framed home, literally a glass box, featured a four-foot module to the windows, which I echoed in the counter's display niches. We converted the former powder room into a walk-in, refrigerated wine room. The breakfast table is a suspended piece of glass, supported by an I-beam structure and cantilevered out from the wall.

FACING PAGE TOP: This home is situated on a ridge, cantilevered off both sides on massive I-beams. The peninsula mirrors this, floating four feet across the window and five feet out into the room. The National Kitchen & Bath Association recognized the kitchen's suspended configuration as the Best Overall Kitchen Winner of that year.

FACING PAGE BOTTOM: Rich kitchen details include African ribbon mahogany cabinets with caramelized-bamboo panels, a freestanding copper sink and countertops made of either mother-of-pearl inlaid concrete or hand-cast glass over flamed copper.

Photographs by Roger Turk

"When we describe how we want our home to look, we are actually describing, in an oblique way, how we want it to feel."

—Richard Landon

TOP: Two chefs get two cooking stations: One uses magnetic induction; the other, gas. By designing a cabinet-clad hood, the openness of this kitchen to the surrounding living spaces has a more aesthetic than functional feel.
Photograph by Roger Turk

BOTTOM: Good interior design responds to the site. Adding a corridor with flanking windows and relites brightens the interior of this classic bungalow and connects the kitchen to the pocket backyard.
Photograph by Roger Turk

FACING PAGE: A Rebecca Bergsma hand-cast glass countertop pairs with a Julie Wawirka cast bronze sink while the pocketing mirror connects the bath to lake views from both the sink and the shower next to the tub. The texture is provided by the marble veining, window coverings, hand-cast sink and glass counter, glass-bead pendant lights, convex profile of the cabinet doors—all work together to create softness in a room full of marble and glass.
Photograph by Mike Nakamura

Walter Gordinier Studios, LLC

Portland, Oregon

"Fine art concepts open the envelopes in the artist's mind to dissolve conventional barriers of thinking."

—Walter Gordinier

ABOVE: As a glass artist, I have the opportunity to create authentic works of art that change with the time of day, read powerfully from a distance and up close and can be touched, even walked upon if necessary. The 40-foot wall of eight-foot-high cast glass panels is in the library at Pacific University. The visual approach incorporates tree trunks, branches and the human figure. The imagery is a result of a stacked composition of pre-selected shapes of color that echo the campus community.
Photograph by Walter Gordinier

FACING PAGE: Homeowners in Hawaii wanted their three-story staircase to be more than functional—they wanted a work of art. Inspired by the bright, distinctive colors associated with Hawaii, I cast pie-shaped paintings to operate as structural material so that art could dictate the flow up and down the steps.
Photograph by Tom Cinquini

"I see no artistic value to arbitrate with concepts that don't elevate my thinking."

—Walter Gordinier

ABOVE: The painting is part of a series commissioned by the Gamma Knife Center, a non-invasive brain surgery center in Portland, Oregon. The painting was inspired by the surgical procedure. To achieve the visual topography, I arranged a composition of the raw cold glass in a manner that allowed it to fall and slump within itself. Artistically, my work is abstract expressionism.

FACING PAGE TOP: Balancing architecture with engineering requirements and the desired aesthetic is a welcome challenge. As a painting in triplicate, the castings were placed to serve as a ceiling and function as a bridge. As quoted by a collector, "Walter has an amazing combination of gifts to provide certified structural integrity to the beauty of every painting."

FACING PAGE BOTTOM: Casting is all about strokes of cold glass being stacked, layered, unstacked, re-arranged and re-stacked—layer upon layer of what I see as a color palate of frozen pieces of geometry. At close range, all layers are seen, edges are exposed, depth is felt.
Photographs by Walter Gordinier

"I'm a colorist, a purist at heart."

—Walter Gordinier

ABOVE: The gill-like protrusion of cast glass is the tremendous impact of the main entrance. Six recessed coffers were installed, and we set the glass on placement Vs that push out 10 inches from the wall, lighting the top and bottom. From either direction, then, the experience is different. Arranging, disarranging, rearranging. Every canvas is a highly complex order of geometry in stacking color fields, intricate areas of thinly veiled to bold strikes of color.
Photograph by Walter Gordinier and Tom Cinquini

FACING PAGE: These architectural elements serve as a room divider providing privacy without blocking natural light. I'm always involved with architects, developers and interior designers to ensure that the placement is perfect. Through experience, I have an acquired impression of what each piece of glass will become and of how the glass expresses itself. I simply allow the nature of the glass to complete the piece on its own terms.
Photograph by Walter Gordinier

BELLAN SHOPWORKS

Seattle, Washington

"The full-service cabinet and furniture shop allows us to help owners realize their true vision— providing unsurpassed personal attention to detail and quality."

—Michael Bellan

ABOVE LEFT: Amazingly comfortable to sit in, this dramatic chair was designed by Michael Bellan and incorporates a steel support and design detail with the beauty of finished teak.
Photograph courtesy of Bellan Shopworks

ABOVE RIGHT: This modernist home, designed by Suyama Peterson Deguchi, features dark stained-walnut cabinets that provide a warm backdrop and graceful contrast to the other materials. The kitchen is very European in its styling, maximizing simplicity—clean and simple with no visible hardware.
Photograph by Robert Pisano Photography

FACING PAGE: Bellan Shopworks is housed in this Michael Bellan-designed office building in the trendy neighborhood of Georgetown. Rusted Cor-Ten steel, coupled with wood siding and a beautiful pinewood pivot door for entry to the office, make for a dramatic streetside display.
Photograph by Bellan Shopworks

"It is critical that the custom cabinetry and furniture integrate seamlessly with the room design and provide that final detail to truly make a place 'home.'"

—Michael Bellan

ABOVE: This substantial remodel, designed by Bohlin Cywinski Jackson, retained the footprint and modern sensibility of the original mid-century structure while creating an exuberant, light-filled home for a young family. Teak cabinetry and stainless-steel countertops with integrated sinks are beautiful and practical. A teak dining nook tucked to the side with a sly window to the home's entry provides a fun place for casual dining and for kids to join in meal preparation.
Photograph by Nic Lehoux Photography

FACING PAGE TOP: The owners of the traditional home wanted a gathering place for the entire family. The beautiful Northwest fir patinas to a rich reddish brown over time. The drawer boxes are made of nine-ply Baltic birch, making them almost as beautiful inside as the cabinetry exteriors. Soft close glides complete the functionality of such a lovely yet friendly space for the active family.
Photograph by Tucker English Photography

FACING PAGE BOTTOM: Our custom woodwork shop offers a full range of services, including fabricating, finishing and installing custom cabinetry—for kitchens, baths, laundry, media centers and wine rooms—as well as custom millwork such as fireplace detail, specialized custom closet interiors and the implementation of custom furniture designs.
Left & middle photographs by Paul Warchol, Warchol Photography
Right photograph by Tucker English Photography

"I prefer to talk about homes as places where real life happens rather than creating the next great photo opportunity."

—Steven Hensel

elements of design

In 1978 Steven Hensel stepped onto the world's stage of design. His designs and artwork began to appear throughout Seattle. Early on, his studio produced hand-painted textiles for architects and interior designers. Wall coverings, woven textiles and furniture soon joined his repertoire, spreading his work across the United States. In the late 1980s Steven began to offer residential and commercial interior design services, and when Hensel Design Studios opened its doors in 1996, the quality of interiors, furniture and textiles was elevated.

Steven has never limited his visionary interior landscape. His projects have spanned from Seattle to Dallas, San Francisco to Hawaii, including an impressive roster of CEOs from national companies, community leaders and many notable individuals. A U.S. embassy even boasts Hensel's furniture. While being featured in many national publications and winning a number of design awards—including Northwest Design Awards' most first-place wins—Steven also finds time for reciprocity in the design community. He has judged many professional design competitions and was a founding chairperson of the Design Industries Foundation Fighting AIDS (DIFFA) in Seattle. The design world is shifting, and Hensel Design Studios is leading the way.

HENSEL DESIGN STUDIOS

"Striving to blur the lines between indoors and outdoors, one can create a palette based on nature, which is timeless, rather than fleeting trends."

—Steven Hensel

LEFT: The high-rise urban sanctuary began as an empty shell of 2,750 square feet and was transformed into a sleek, modern home of extraordinary comfort. A water-feature wall in the entry was designed to introduce an aura of serenity amidst the vibrant urban setting. The commodious entry hall also serves as a gallery for several of the owner's sculptures and paintings.

FACING & PREVIOUS PAGES: An unusual fossil stone was used as flooring throughout—its inclusion on the terrace helps to blur the delineation of indoor-outdoor space. Walnut-paneled walls and cabinetry were designed to provide a sense of serene continuity while cleverly concealing many features such as televisions, vents, controls, even the pullout cooktop hood. In fact, the kitchen area seems more akin to a swank lounge as it opens to the larger living area. Glowing resin panels lift to reveal the working kitchen elements that are hidden beneath. Controlled bursts of color are found within the custom rug along with custom pillows, accessories and artwork.
Photographs by William Wright

"I believe a home has the potential to be welcoming, comfortable, functional, luxurious and unpretentious, all at the same time."

—Steven Hensel

ABOVE: Located on the south slope of Seattle's Queen Anne Hill, the home was once owned by the Northwest's legendary interior designer Jean Jongeward. With all due respect to Jongeward, the new owners' desires, active family lifestyle and eclectic collection of artwork became top priority for the new design. With the new furnishings, many custom-designed specifically for the home, a casual, comfortable yet sophisticated ambience was achieved.

FACING PAGE: A spectacular terrace facing the quintessential Space Needle view features a dining experience that incorporates lighting, music and flowing outdoor draperies. Though luxurious, the home is never ostentatious and is as unique as its owners.
Photographs by Alex Hayden

"Those who enter my studio have their own distinctive qualities, lifestyles and desires. I make sure that their homes reflect that."

—Steven Hensel

ABOVE: The living room was divided into two zones. Four large-scale armchairs that circle a coffee table anchor the steel-clad fireplace at one end. The city view end of the room sports a curved sofa that wraps around one of the custom tables crafted from steel and bronze. A game table completes the composition and is a favorite spot for cozy family meals.

FACING PAGE: The homeowners lead a busy life with two successful careers, two teenage daughters, a dog and a guinea pig. Spaces perform multiple tasks that easily accommodate intimate dinners for four, dinner parties for 12 or cocktail parties for 150. The traditional 1920s' home was updated with a modern approach to furnishings, palette and fabrics. Textures were favored over pattern, which allows for a calm tableau. The art collection and furnishings coexist without competing.
Photographs by Alex Hayden

RIGHT & FACING PAGE: The high-rise condominium, a quarter of a century old, was a maze of small, dated rooms, many with enormous unused, unappreciated window seats. As the couple had little need for four bedrooms, a new plan was developed to enhance their lifestyle. The couple's list of priorities included plenty of entertaining space, adding storage and work space, the ability to occasionally accommodate overnight guests and control excessive heat and glare from the southern exposure as well as opening up the fantastic views. With just over 2,000 square feet to work with, the home's perception was changed to an open, loft-like space stretching 50 feet in length. A warm slate was chosen to pave the entire space with the exception of the master bedroom; this natural flooring visually connects two exterior decks with the interior space. Each of the three window seats gained a new function. In the living area, a custom sofa and side platforms added precious square footage to the room. The dining area gained a large steel and wood sideboard surrounded by plants. The third window seat sports a large work table that doubles as dining space for the couple. A home office with many file drawers and computer equipment is concealed in the backside of the kitchen cabinetry. Many of the pieces of furniture were designed specifically for the space by the interior designer, including the bronze dining table with a cast-glass top and the china cabinet with inlaid details. A mural was commissioned to cover a wall in the living room, which evokes an ethereal setting in China.

Photographs by Thomas Barwick

RIGHT: Floor-to-ceiling pivoting panels of stained fir—also used for the built-in cabinetry—were employed throughout the space in lieu of doors. The panels fold neatly into shallow niches or when closed take on the appearance of a paneled wall; they are held in place with magnetic devices. This system was used at both entries to the kitchen, the master suite, the guest closet and the utility room. A very large panel in the library appears to be a wall but can roll to close the space off for privacy when used as a guest room. Central air conditioning was cleverly and discreetly added through the library cabinetry and soffits. The master bath was reconfigured to allow for a large shower that doubles as a steam room. A walk-in closet and built-in dressers were added to greatly increase clothing storage.

FACING PAGE: The kitchen was enlarged and now opens to the remarkable view. A bar area was added for entertaining purposes as well as ample wine storage. A steam oven and walk-in pantry greatly enhance its functionality. Low-voltage lighting with dimming capabilities dramatically highlight the home's artwork, furnishings and architecture. State-of-the-art window coverings have a reflective coating on the outside to deflect heat and glare while a darker tone faces the interior to allow the occupant a lightly veiled view of the city, bay and mountains—even on the sunniest of days.
Photographs by Thomas Barwick

KAINDL GLASS ART

Kirkland, Washington

"I strive to create art glass that is both evocative and inspiring."

—Robert Kaindl

ABOVE: The inspiration for the Signature Collection was organic forms, specifically sea life. I incorporate the classic Murano glassblowing techniques while infusing my work with an edgy yet organic style. I created the Amber Gold Celebration Series chandelier installation for a client's private compound; it's a great example of perfect balance and symmetry. The chandelier weighs 400 pounds yet is suspended by a single cable. I describe my chandelier installations as a series of "visual contradictions"—they appear to be floating, yet the average weight of a chandelier is over 500 pounds.

FACING PAGE: The Celebration Chandelier Series is created exclusively with transparent colors. If you have bubbles or flaws in the glass they will be apparent. I am a perfectionist. I love the beauty of pure glass without inclusions, each delicate, uninterrupted translucent piece. The effort is certainly painstaking but worth it. In a private automobile museum—the collection valued at 280 million dollars—the taillight red Celebration Series chandelier installation is 22-by-12 feet and weighs a staggering 6,200 pounds. The chandelier series is fully functional, lit from within, which provides the fiery backdrop for the American hotrod muscle cars.
Photographs by Robert Kaindl

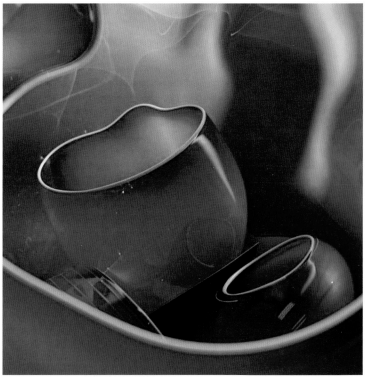

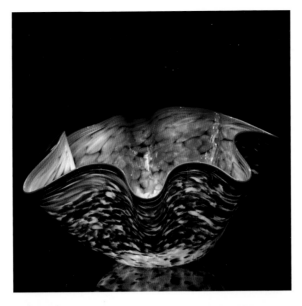

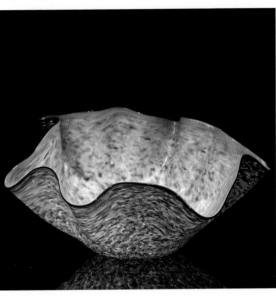

RIGHT: Ostrea, one of my most substantial series, is based on the Pacific Northwest Oyster. I wanted to bring broader awareness to our fragile ecosystems. As a native of the Pacific Northwest, I support numerous foundations to maintain the health of the ecology. Although beautiful creatures, oysters are not vibrantly colored, so I created several color stories based on either aquatic species or iconic works by master impressionists, such as Monet's *Water-Lily Pond*.

FACING PAGE: The Anthias Collection was named for the reef-dwelling, brilliantly colored fish. I created several series based on a fascination with aquatic species and a passion for the preservation of their habitats. Lighting is very important—hence the glass must be flawless. I utilize both gold and platinum in this series to mimic the prismatic sheen of the water and scales of the Anthias.
Photographs by Robert Kaindl

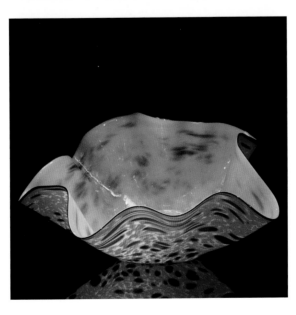

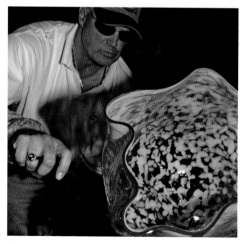

"The end of the journey is always a remarkable moment."

—Robert Kaindl

RIGHT: The RK Signature Collection is at once modern and classic. This was formerly one of John Wayne's Californian homes, now owned by the owners of the Beverly Hills Four Seasons Hotel. Eleven feet tall, this masterpiece has hundreds of tendrils that are punctuated at the tip with hand-sculpted giant irises in the fashion of the classic Lalique crystal.

FACING PAGE: All of my creations are custom; each piece is hand-blown, -sculpted or -cast by me and my team. Glassblowing is very physical work, and the scale of work for which I am known is very demanding. I do not create visual obstructions; the art glass needs to punctuate the space. The moment of completion is really an emotional moment for both me and my client. There are always tears, always champagne—really, 100 percent of my collectors have become our friends.

Photographs by Robert Kaindl

"Understanding the relevance of space is essential."

—Robert Kaindl

ABOVE: The inspiration for this gorgeous Wall Sea Shape Series was several sea creatures, including mollusks, jellyfish and sea anemones. Glass in its fluid state is malleable, supple and translucent, not bound by form. In creating these beautiful and unusual shapes, I let the shape come out of the glass. As these amazing creatures move so gracefully through the water, they take on millions of shapes—this series was meant to capture motion.

FACING PAGE: Again, the installation is the final expression of my vision as a glass artist. I try to capture movement with spacing and by utilizing different elevations. Art glass collectors Jim and CK Coles wanted an art glass installation that was very prominent yet traditional. Based on the man o' war, the shapes undulate along the wall, casting a shadow that is delicate, fluid and elegant. I believe that art, and particularly art glass, provides an amazing experience because it is constantly changing with the light.
Photographs by Robert Kaindl

"I would like to make something that's never been made before."

—Evert Sodergren

ABOVE: The curved rib design of the bench creates interplay with light and shadow. Stretched leather crosses the seat so that a true Viking influence is captured. The strength of rosewood lamination makes possible this design aesthetic of delicate curved pieces, demonstrating a passion for experimentation.

FACING PAGE: Hardwood and brass combine to create the Family Tree Coffee Table that showcases the vertically oriented wood grain. The 230 rings of 1/16-inch-thick strips of walnut endgrain represent 230 combined years that Sodergrens have been making furniture.
Photographs by Kay Walsh

"A good craftsman is not one who never makes mistakes but one who knows what to do with them."

—Evert Sodergren

ABOVE: Making the conversion from side table to table for four was an idea in transitions. The gate legs swing out, and the top flips open. Madrona burl panels and custom brass hardware bring detailing to the forefront.
Photographs by Kay Walsh

FACING PAGE: Designed in 1957, the chair has delicate-looking thin legs; but the meeting of four wooden parts in an x-configuration is a design element made possible by laminating a 3/16-inch birch panel inside the walnut pieces of the chair's sides. This "bone" provides both strength and unique visual interest. The comfort of the chair is partly achieved by the hinged seat back, which pivots to match the person's seating position. It was partly inspired by the sculptural armrests on a vintage Swedish chair passed down the Sodergren family line. The challenge was to produce a unique chair that would be too difficult to reproduce in the average 1950s' wood shop.
Photograph courtesy of Sodergren Furniture

"The designer shouldn't strive for artistic pieces, but rather well-designed, well-crafted furniture."

—Evert Sodergren

ABOVE LEFT: This Knight's Bench is made with bamboo and eastern maple. The seat and legs are laminated curved bamboo made in a form with solid sculpted wood feet and spacer. The custom seat cushion is attached with Velcro straps. Great visual interest comes with this extremely light-weight occasional seating piece.
Photograph by Kay Walsh

ABOVE RIGHT: The Tribal Stool is an extra portable seat for a person who wants to work or play with objects on the floor. When not in use, it becomes a sculptural art item on the shelf. Inspired by a similar African piece, the stool was traditionally carved from a single, solid tree stump and carried to gatherings with the thin seat piece under the arm. Here, the legs are hand-sculpted walnut joined with ebony mortise plugs to the seat, which is a walnut lamination, made in a form.
Photograph by Kay Walsh

FACING PAGE: The large tansu, crafted in the tradition of the Asian tansu, is a free-standing chest with sliding cabinet doors and 10 drawers, clad with protective handmade hardware around its corners and edges. The use of asymmetry in design plays with the division of space in each row of drawers. Repairing vintage Asian tansus provided the inspiration for this design.
Photograph courtesy of Sodergren Furniture

ABOVE: Scandinavian influences started showing up in the late 1960s and 1970s, such as the Dot Tables, originally made as exhibition pieces. Circles add decorative interest to the tables, set atop laminated arcs for the base.

Photographs courtesy of Sodergren Furniture

FACING PAGE: A contemporary adaptation of the Asian tansu, the chest has showcase veneer on the top panel, bordered by an ebony-inlaid frame. This model features ebony corner details and slatted side and door panels. The medallion door hardware and the side lifting handles are both custom made with oxidized brass. The side lifting handles follow the Asian design—a bamboo pole would go through either end for easier moving.

Photographs by Kay Walsh

GULASSA & CO.

Seattle, Washington

"Patience, trust and keeping an open mind are paramount to achieving a rewarding result."

—Barrett Sheppard

ABOVE & FACING PAGE: We hope people take pleasure in seeing something that catches them by surprise. Our tchotchka, which covers every surface of the workshop, is kind of a microcosm of our work at large: David always wanted to do it all. David's innate talent was his intuitive eye and his ability to incorporate the familiar or the discarded into something new and surprisingly beautiful. The snapshot above is of David Gulassa, who passed away in 2001. We have tried to create a great place for inspiration, and we've been told that there is something magical in the air here. *Photographs by Stefan Gulassa*

"Having passion for a project is contagious—it filters down to everyone."

—Barrett Sheppard

RIGHT: David and Stefan Gulassa designed the DG Dining Chair piece for our Works furniture line. Made of walnut, blackened steel and leather, it's the intersection of design, materials and proportion—all equally important to the final design.

FACING PAGE: The electrified chandelier raises and lowers at the touch of a fingertip. Counterweights hold the piece in place, and polarized components complete the electric circuit, creating a wireless light. The hardware, in essence, becomes the focal point by exemplifying stellar craftsmanship. Every shop artisan brings a unique skill set and an individual perspective to our collaborative work.
Photographs by Stefan Gulassa

"Beauty is our catalyst, so craftsmanship and integrity must be found in each project."

—Barrett Sheppard

ABOVE & FACING PAGE: *Lebeg*, created by Ann Gardner, is a floating sculpture—the name means a "slight movement in air." Each of the nine pods is 12 feet long and weighs 200 pounds. The light catches on the mosaic tiles as the sculpture rotates. This is the great thing about art: You can see the beauty here, even if you don't have the words to describe it. The piece really represents the fundamental satisfaction behind the business: working with an amazing group of wonderful and talented people. It truly is the best job in the world—most of the time.
Photographs by Stefan Gulassa

ELEMENTS GLASS, LLC

Portland, Oregon

"Glass is one of the few materials that has its own movement, that can suddenly lead you in a new creative direction while working it."

—Ian Gilula

ABOVE: Glassmaking is challenging because glass is not an easy material to manipulate—it doesn't really want to be anything. But that, of course, is the fun. When we started Elements Glass, we wanted to create art with high intrigue. This work was commissioned for a company that creates the dye injected into cells for cell photography. We wanted to create a piece that was an expression of molecular photography and that mimicked an element of the natural habitat of the company's location—the local coastal cypress tree. Twenty feet tall, dropping from the second floor staircase—that certainly makes an exciting statement. Art by Ian Gilula.

FACING PAGE: *The Eternal Light* was created for a synagogue in St. Louis, Missouri. Weighing a ton and lit by LED lighting, the sculpture consists of 400 ribbons of interwoven glass. The piece hangs over the Torah arc, and its manifestation of light is of religious note, for light plays a significant role in Judaism. The idea was to have a stunning, glowing object that breathes life into the entryway. Art by Ian Gilula and Aaron Frankel.
Photographs by Spencer Paul

"Glass art, with its radiance of color, uniqueness of form and organic luminosity, allows each viewer to be swept into a singular, soulful experience."

—Ian Gilula

ABOVE: In the grand stairwell of the Nines, a luxury Portland hotel, hangs *Birdsong*, a 35-foot waterfall of glass. Conceptual artist Melody Owen developed the idea of taking the sonograms of endangered Pacific Northwest birds and translating the songs into a translucent representative of local concerns. Ian Gilula then took the conceptual images and translated and fabricated them into this three-dimensional sculpture. Art by Melody Owen, translated and fabricated by Ian Gilula.

FACING PAGE: The owner of a multimillion-dollar yacht commissioned us to create eight sculptures. This was a site-specific design that needed to be permanently fixed to the boat. While the stair-side sculpture represents a large, ridged raindrop for liquidity, the opposing countertop pieces symbolize male and female figures. Art by Ian Gilula.
Photographs by Spencer Paul

"Glass offers the unique opportunity to create an object that captures a moment in time."

—Aaron Frankel

LEFT: Having seen our *Eternal Light*, an organization commissioned us for a radiant sculpture that would represent the color spectrum in a double-helix fashion. This work reflects movement, colors and transition. Art by Ian Gilula and Aaron Frankel.

FACING PAGE: Our objective is to create art that offers the opportunity for fascinating dialogue between friends. My orange and yellow *Carnival* vase shows how glass can behave in form and color through a circus motif, allowing for lively conversation. Movement and form drive my heavier translucent piece, showing how balance can play out visually. Aaron Frankel, Elements Glass's other half, designed the Italian-style vase and the opaque piece that offers a crackling rhythm. Between the two of us, glassmaking is shown in all its rich variants. Art by Ian Gilula and Aaron Frankel. *Photographs by Spencer Paul*

Seattle, Washington

"A return to ancient techniques has created a renaissance in carpet weaving."

—Driscoll Robbins

ABOVE: I first went to Asia in 1972 as a child. My parents were well-known antique carpet dealers in San Francisco, and I would spend my career following in their footsteps. This is how you truly develop the sensibility for a subject: spend your life doing it. I'm fascinated by what happens when the old tradition of weaving is blended with modern sensibilities, such as Ariana's carpets, which combine classic patterns with a decorative color palette. They have the look and feel of worn antique rugs but with a modern aesthetic. Each carpet is an exclusive.

FACING PAGE: Woven Legends is famous for weaving carpets with the look and feel of the most desirable antique carpets. They use hand-spun wool and natural dyes and are woven by hand using ancient techniques. Each carpet is distinctive and individually selected based on color, pattern and artistic merit.
Photographs by Marco Prozzo

"Carpet weaving is never static—it is an art form with limitless possibilities."

—Driscoll Robbins

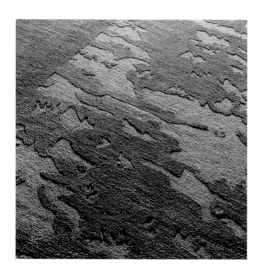

ABOVE LEFT: A renaissance in rug weaving began about 15 years ago, and as a result, producers are encouraged to push the limits of pattern, texture and color. Many of our contemporary patterns are hand-woven in Nepal and designed by prestigious Western designers. Each rug—like the Lapchi Carpet—is woven using the finest hand-spun wool and dyes.

ABOVE MIDDLE: New methods in weaving offer many more choices to the consumer and allow us to work closely with interior designers to achieve subtle variations of color, like in the natural dyes of the Odegard Carpet.

ABOVE RIGHT: Sahar carpets are woven in private homes in Southern Iran. The weavers are given a simple sketch and are free to create as they go. Each carpet is a one-of-a-kind work of art. The brown color in the carpet is un-dyed wool, showing the natural variation of each yarn.

FACING PAGE TOP: Many rugs are used as backdrops to accentuate the artwork and furniture in a room. The Tufenkian Carpet is an example of a surface carpet, allowing the eye to go to other parts of the room.

FACING PAGE BOTTOM: Lapchi is the leader in hand-woven custom carpets. A large part of our business is weaving carpets to specific requirements of size, color, scale and pattern. No company has mastered the technique of custom carpets more then Lapchi.

Photographs by Marco Prozzo

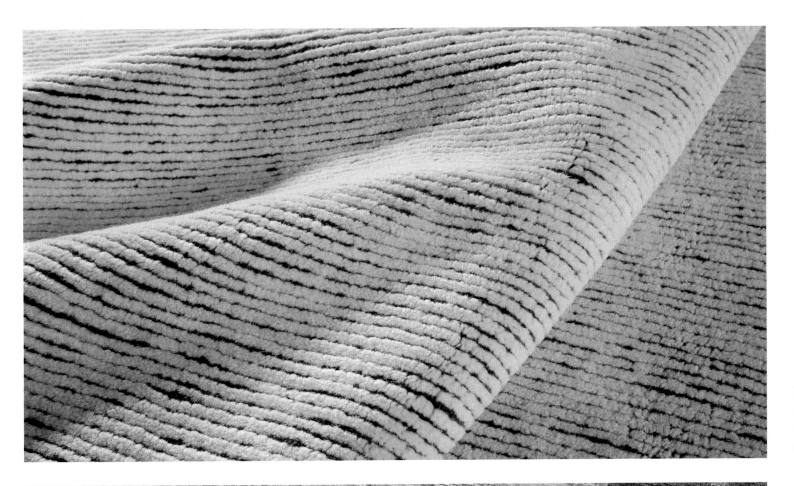

GAGE WINDOW COVERINGS

Bellevue, Washington

"One of the keys to a good end result is integration with the structure; working early on with the architect is necessary to achieve this."

—Mike Gage

ABOVE & FACING PAGE: Over the 20 years that we've been in business, the demand for automated window coverings has skyrocketed. The look is cool, sleek and user-friendly. With proper application and installation, these products can play a heavy hand in the occupants' comfort level. *Photographs courtesy of Gage Window Coverings*

"Years ago people were manually lighting their lamps to control light in their homes until the Edison lightbulb came into use. A hundred years later we surprisingly all too often still manually control exterior light that enters our homes."

—Mike Gage

ABOVE: Having many styles and fabrics to choose from, we can make sure the needs of individual homeowners are met, whether that means sheer window coverings or total blackout options.

FACING PAGE: One of the more sophisticated shading systems is the Lutron QED Roller Shades, which is totally automated and can be easily controlled from anywhere in the structure.

Photographs courtesy of Gage Window Coverings

"Attending to exquisite detail is like knowing the precise number of saffron threads to add to the perfect paella."

—Joel Shepard

ABOVE: The marriage of graphic design and the furniture-maker's art creates a visual poem of celebration—the Anniversary Spirit Vessel. I did an extensive interview with my client, who commissioned the piece as a gift for her husband on their 40th wedding anniversary. Each of the icons represents aspects of the couple's rich and varied lives. In Northwest Native American culture, there is an iconic myth that tells of Raven stealing the sun, and so the image circles the vessel.
Photograph by Joel Shepard

FACING PAGE: A renowned author desired a multipurpose cabinet that could incorporate 19 distinct functions while adhering to the classic Biedermeier style and detailing. Incorporating the myriad contemporary functions into the classic design was certainly challenging—I had to find and adapt all of the hardware to fit the needs while sourcing the stunning veneer for all the outside surfaces. Designed in collaboration with architect Norm Sandler and designer Elizabeth Beers.
Photograph by Gary Vannest

ABOVE: I immerse myself into a design until it begins to speak to me. From then on, it's a collaboration between me and creative forces that I cannot begin to fathom. The Biedermeier cabinet is a superb piece of work—one of those projects that dictates what it wants you to do as you go. The author, again, required a stand-up writing desk with 21st-century technology but loved the classic style of the Old World. The contemporary functionality remains hidden behind classic detailing until called to action. Within moments, false drawer fronts become a keyboard tray, the intricate parquet-floor "ballroom" folds back to reveal the laptop computer, and a side panel pops open to expose a printer/fax, all of which allow him wireless communication and information sharing anywhere in the world. The paneled mahogany door at the back of the "ballroom" opens to two trompe l'oeil rooms with a gold-framed photo of his literary hero, Noël Coward. For the author, this Alice in Wonderland-like cabinet perfectly captures his style and personality.

Photographs by Rebecca Nelson

FACING PAGE TOP: The '40 Ford Woodie Station Wagon piece was commissioned by a client for her husband's birthday. He has an extensive collection of superb cars—one of only 20 people in the world who have both a Mercedes 300SL Gullwing Coupe and a 300SL Roadster! His '40 Woodie, however, is his favorite driving car and was used to carry his daughter to her wedding. I had the coupe version of this beauty when I was a kid, so I was well aware of every curve and detail and just how the front fenders feel and where the sweet spot for sitting is so you don't slide off. This was part of a long series of "treasure boxes" I made. The top is hinged and lockable, and there is a tray inside for multiple layers of treasures. The real car is painted almost this natural color of purpleheart wood.

Photograph by Ken Wagner

FACING PAGE BOTTOM: All of the homeowners' entertainment "stuff" had to fit into this cabinet, which, in turn, had to fit into the niche to the side of their fireplace. When not in use, all the gizmos had to be hidden away, and when in use, had to be visible, listenable and controllable from anywhere in their great room. Adapting classic Japanese furniture design to incorporate modern conveniences, I was truly inspired by the richness of details in everything Japanese.

Photographs by Rain Grimes

MARK NEWMAN DESIGN IN WOOD

"In a good piece of furniture, there is no distinction between form and function."

—Mark Newman

ABOVE: At heart, I am both a designer and a craftsman. The Elizabeth bedroom suite is a piece that grew out of both my love of presenting a beautiful piece of wood in a simple form and solving a need for the user. Crafted from sapele and wenge, the bed has four drawers beneath for storage, making it perfectly suited to modern condo living.

FACING PAGE: The Elizabeth bureau is actually a remarkably complex sculptural piece. The drawers have no box around them; instead, they are supported by a skeletal frame that is revealed only when the drawer is opened. I discovered the method of construction, virtually unused in modern woodworking, when I was repairing an old antique. A cylindrical rail guides the drawers, cutting down the friction, which means that, even though the drawer is quite wide and the pull is way over in one corner, it still opens very smoothly. This piece would not exist had I not stumbled across that antique. The optional mirror ties the design to the bed headboard while providing both a full length and vanity mirror.
Photographs by Joel Newman

"Fine craftsmanship speaks for itself."

—Mark Newman

ABOVE: The koa slab had been in storage for 30 years when it was brought to me. The client wanted me to cut it into boards for a smaller work, but my argument for using it as a single piece won out. Set atop an ash base, the naturally bark-edged koa wood is a perfect counterpoint to the smooth support.
Photograph by Joel Newman

FACING PAGE TOP & BOTTOM LEFT: I call the piece the Garlic Table because the bases and the carving reflect the three garlic-shaped chandeliers that hang over it. The table was built to suit the clients' lifestyle of entertaining. The three tables, including the drop-leaf side table, can be connected or separated at the S-curved tongue-and-groove joint. This allows the room to be configured to seat from 4 to 22 guests. The Garlic Table is a good example of a project that had to meet several, disparate design criteria.
Photographs by Mark Stein Photography

FACING PAGE BOTTOM RIGHT: Condo living also drove the Jeff Lamb-designed Tea Table. Made of wenge, the table uses a pinwheel design, where each leg is mitered into the frame at the top. Custom woodworking, in the end, must reflect the people who use it.
Photograph by Mark Stein Photography

SMJ Studio

Seattle, Washington

"Fabric is a very challenging creative medium, but once you understand how it moves, the possibilities are really quite endless."

—Sara Johnson

ABOVE: The chaise lounge's slipcover represents nearly 20 years of experience in the complex art of patternmaking. By applying techniques from my education in apparel design, I'm able to create slipcovers that naturally embrace and complement many unique furniture forms.

FACING PAGE: Luxurious bedding is one of the highlights of our repertoire, which also includes custom window treatments, cushions, pillows and other soft interior elements. From chic glamour to subtle sophistication, each piece is personally manufactured to suit people's individual needs and desires. To produce beautiful products that function flawlessly, my team and I address the technical demands without sacrificing aesthetics; that innovative approach has earned us a local and global clientele.
Photographs by David Bell

"For designing a room, drapery is often a great place to start because it can make a dramatic statement. This can often serve as a point of inspiration for subsequent design decisions."

—Sara Johnson

ABOVE: It takes a considerable amount of skill to address the challenges that can arise when designing for complex architectural shells, including historical homes and commercial renovations. Each project is a unique mathematical and creative sewing feat that requires extraordinary attention to detail. In addition to sourcing the finest fabrics from around world, we have solid connections with some of Seattle's most talented artisans for upholstery and metalwork.
Photographs by David Bell

FACING PAGE TOP: Our close working relationship with SkB Architects allows us to create amazing spaces as well as write exact specifications and help solve difficult design issues.
Photograph by John Granen

FACING PAGE BOTTOM: As the exclusive sewing workroom for Hensel Design Studios, we have pushed beyond the apparent limitations of time, fabric and structure in order to achieve many gorgeous, award-winning spaces.
Photograph by Alex Hayden

STEVE JENSEN

Seattle, Washington

"Tapping into ancient archetypes speaks to universality and timelessness."

—Steve Jensen

ABOVE: A Viking must die with a sword in his hand to go to Valhalla. The carved cedar, cast acrylic and fishbone piece from Norway is part of my Voyager series, which comes from my experiences with the deaths of loved ones. This ship was burned to signify a traditional Viking funeral.

FACING PAGE: The carving "Red Swirls" is an abstract with oceanic aesthetics that encompasses my Norwegian heritage and our broader sensibilities. The piece is 60 by 48 inches and is carved from recycled wood.
Photographs by Linda Young

"At some point, you get to a place where you realize that life is really short, and I've tried to explore and express that through my art."

—Steve Jensen

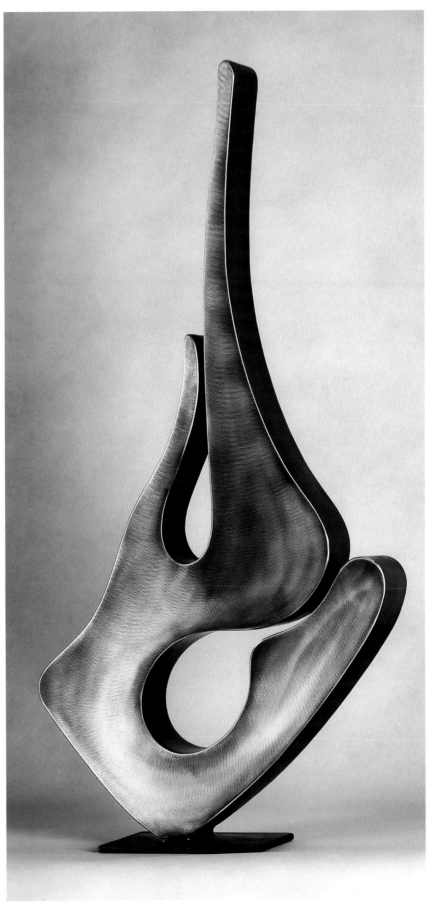

RIGHT: "Bronze Sailboat" plays to Nordic mythologies. Death is the one final thing we all have in common, and the universal image of the boat symbolizes this voyage.

FACING PAGE TOP: When I work with themes of loss, I feel transported to another place where the artist is asked to be both craftsman and mortician. "Carved Canoes" is a product of this, and to maintain the Norwegian tradition, all the carvings are made of fallen wood.

FACING PAGE BOTTOM: An abstract compass on a roadside roundabout in Bend, Oregon, "Compass" is aluminum and stands 144 inches tall. The piece expresses the often-whimsical nature of voyages.

Photographs by Linda Young

266 perspectives on design

"Your home reflects you, a person of independence."

—Brian Kemnitz

ABOVE: The options in color are infinite; reaching beyond simple wall paint is a matter of considering all of the possibilities. We've set up our showroom to bring some of those choices to the forefront. Some 500 sample finishes on multiple surfaces are available throughout—walls, ceilings, trim, doors, cabinets, furniture and much more. We get your mind working in a creative mode so that unique finishes become an extension of you.

FACING PAGE: For a thousand years, Venetian plaster has been a striking way to adorn a wall. The polished plaster is cool to the touch and lends itself to the Old World Italian way of crafting a home's aesthetics. This type of finish adapts and defines to all forms of interior design—there are so many looks and styles that break the traditional mold of simple wall paint.
Photographs by Rebecca Zurstadt

"Each project presents a unique combination of opportunities."

—Kenneth Philp

living the elements

chapter five

Landscape Architecture requires comfort with many architectural styles because those elements of the structure help inform the landscape design. The style of the home infuses and inspires the landscape. Gardens, however, can be forgivingly eclectic. A garden may have a classical theme, for instance, but unrelated nooks and crannies can exist, enticing the visitor. This serendipitous and analytical approach to landscape design is very apparent in the work of Kenneth Philp Landscape Architects. Emphasizing three essential aspects of design, principal Kenneth Philp and associate Scott Holsapple consider the architectural style of the home, the inherent qualities of the site and, of course, the personality and vision of the homeowners.

Throughout its progression, each project presents a unique combination of opportunities. Ken's process-oriented design approach is flexible and adaptable, allowing the firm to fully address the complexities and opportunities of individual projects and respond in kind. With this tailored process, gardens of distinction can be created that express these three essential aspects of design. Gardens should have a sense of arrival and of simple procession as one is drawn through; spaces or rooms should be inviting. Ken's personalized process involves translating architecture into this procession in a diverse and alluring manner, evoking the sense that "it is a natural fit."

KENNETH PHILP LANDSCAPE ARCHITECTS

ABOVE: Layering landscape architecture with deeply textural tapestries of planting can turn nooks into magical places. The warmth of the playful shadows cast from Allium bulbs project childlike silhouettes against the stone veneer. The palette has a Mediterranean feel, working wonders as a backdrop to the Lavender.

FACING PAGE: Seasons dramatically affect the plant palette in the Pacific Northwest. Since this region only receives four to five warm months a year, an understanding of climate and microclimate is vital. Our job is to create long-lasting and ever-evolving interest year-round. In working with the client, we envisioned a park-like setting weaving the house and terraces into the landscape. The space has a wonderful aspect, and we knew the children would be running across the grassy meadow, so keeping the lawn areas open and flowing was essential. One of the great delights of our profession is watching families enjoy these spaces as they take shape over the years. As the landscape matures and begins to evolve, the intent of our work can be seen. Architecture by Gelotte Hommas Architecture.

PREVIOUS PAGES: The owner played a great role in the design of the terrace. She had some very specific ideas of what she wanted, and so our process adapted to her goals. The elegant space feels somewhat classical with water spilling from the arbor and a balustrade with that mysterious door—a very processional garden. Classical columns and the building façade blend with eclectic landscaping for a very welcoming yet private garden room. The journey into the home and garden begins as you pass through the portal of the front entry stair. Architecture by Robert Maloney Architects.
Photographs by Steve Young

"Landscape architecture is the discovery and recognition of place."

—Kenneth Philp

ABOVE & FACING PAGE: Sometimes you begin with sites that are blank slates, but others begin as beautiful forests. Puget Sound and Lake Washington were both crafted by the last glaciation, carved from a wooded lowland into an intricate series of waterways. In more recent history, properties along the shores of these waterways have become very desirable. On these slopes and terraces, both manmade and natural, homes and gardens have appeared along the water's edge in harmony and conflict with nature's intent. Previously, this lot was a sliding plane, but you would never know the complexity of engineering behind its design by simple observation. The home reflects the client's roots in the Midwest and shares characteristics of Taliesin, a Frank Lloyd Wright work. The garden is an eclectic landscape with seasonal color and soft flowing drifts. In our design, the personality of the owner really comes through in the playful rhythms of the plant compositions. Architecture by Olson Sundberg Kundig Allen Architects.
Photographs by Steve Young

"One of my greatest delights is coming back years later and seeing the evolution that has taken place."

—Kenneth Philp

ABOVE: Urban rooftops present great opportunities for the introduction of green spaces. The private rooftop courtyard of this townhome and condominium was built to LEED Gold certification, 14 stories above the streets of Seattle. The use of low-impact development standards and a variety of recycled materials forges a new and contextually relevant model for sustainable design. Architecture by Mithun.

FACING PAGE: The homeowners did not want any lawn but did want a welcoming courtyard. To keep the pedestrian circulation in context and cadence with the architecture, a contemporary, geometric design was conceived using emerald and lime green Irish and Scottish Moss. The rusted drain grate adds contrast to the light and dark colors of the moss. In keeping with the textural quality of the board-form concrete walls, an evergreen huckleberry is placed as the centerpiece in a ceramic urn with ornamental grass. As a whole, the home has a nice, modular, contemporary Pacific Northwest Asian theme to the design. Architecture by Rex Hohlbein Architects.
Photographs by Steve Young

"With thoughtful site planning, architecture and the garden design are drawn together and intimately connected."

—Kenneth Philp

LEFT & FACING PAGE: At the base of a stretch of steep bluffs along the shores of Puget Sound, the home was knocked from its foundation by a series of hillslope failures and landslide events nearly a decade ago. The process of unearthing and restoration was painstaking and took nearly five years to accomplish. Current site conditions give no indication of the previous devastation. The waterfront side is now a rustic, beautiful coastal setting seemingly far removed from the nearby city. The sometimes harsh salt-sprayed environment requires a hardier planting palette than most other gardens. To survive direct exposure to salt and prevailing winds, site planning preparation needed to adhere to a different set of rules. Large stones were used to visually connect one to the expansive panoramic aspect of the site while also serving to add stability to the slope. We used predominantly local stone such as granite for its regional look, providing dramatic and natural shapes. The courtyard gardens in the upland portion of the garden are much more formal. Situated directly off the dining room, these garden spaces were crafted as extensions of the interior where more refined materials blend gradually into the natural setting. The garden as a whole is a whimsical and natural retort to the earlier ruin that devastated the area. Architecture by AOME Architects.

Photographs by Steve Young

"Flexibility and adaptability are requisite tools of the landscape architect."

—Kenneth Philp

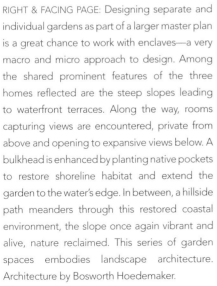

RIGHT & FACING PAGE: Designing separate and individual gardens as part of a larger master plan is a great chance to work with enclaves—a very macro and micro approach to design. Among the shared prominent features of the three homes reflected are the steep slopes leading to waterfront terraces. Along the way, rooms capturing views are encountered, private from above and opening to expansive views below. A bulkhead is enhanced by planting native pockets to restore shoreline habitat and extend the garden to the water's edge. In between, a hillside path meanders through this restored coastal environment, the slope once again vibrant and alive, nature reclaimed. This series of garden spaces embodies landscape architecture. Architecture by Bosworth Hoedemaker.
Photographs by Steve Young

D.M. OHASHI LANDSCAPE SERVICES

Issaquah, Washington

"Beauty is often stimulated by the simplest of nature's evolving details."

—David M. Ohashi

ABOVE: Simple details, supplied wholly by nature, lend a distinct elegance to any landscape.

FACING PAGE: Transitions are a critical element of any landscape. The water window frames the tranquil movement from one space to another.
Photographs by Maria Sanchez, Alchemie

"Construction of a landscape project must always be respectful of the design intent."

—David M. Ohashi

ABOVE LEFT: This inside-outside connection celebrates the successful relationship of spaces through masterful use of materials, scale and topography.

ABOVE RIGHT: By integrating organic and modern elements, such as outcrop boulders with concrete, green space is created in an organized manner.

FACING PAGE TOP: At the entry courtyard, the water-feature wall successfully fuses form and function despite a challenging grade change.

FACING PAGE BOTTOM: Clean, simple and elegant materials relate to each other on a basic level yet in a sophisticated manner.
Photographs by Maria Sanchez, Alchemie

"Working with a design team is remarkably similar to relationships found in landscapes; they must function individually and together with a common goal and effect."

—David M. Ohashi

RIGHT: Landscape architecture and organic features work together to seamlessly transition and bridge structure with plant form.
Photograph by Maria Sanchez, Alchemie

FACING PAGE TOP: A dramatic entry pond and the use of stone wall systems play hide-and-seek, piquing guests' curiosity and providing interior privacy.
Photograph courtesy of D.M. Ohashi Landscape Services

FACING PAGE BOTTOM: The geometric runnel connects two bodies of water and distinctly separates outdoor living areas.
Photograph courtesy of D.M. Ohashi Landscape Services

"In their finished form, landscape features often convey simplicity and elegance to the eye, yet the construction process and design phase can be deceptively complex."

—David M. Ohashi

ABOVE: An infinity-edge water feature with vertical plantings frames and extends the view of a distant lake.
Photograph by Maria Sanchez, Alchemie

FACING PAGE TOP: Proportion and placement of wall systems provide screening and frame garden rooms while maintaining multiple perspectives of a water-feature focal point.
Photograph by Ricklee Stone

FACING PAGE BOTTOM: Stones are a natural and organic solution to creating a water source for recirculating water features.
Photograph by Dale Lang, NW Architectural Photography

"The diversity of projects which one builds reflects a commitment to think forward, with an open mind, and challenges a firm in the quest for excellence."

—David M. Ohashi

RIGHT: Dry stack stone walls and steps display the essence of Old World craftsmanship and frame a destination point within the garden.
Photograph by David M. Ohashi

FACING PAGE TOP: Details, defiance and spring color provide articulate definition to this intimate landscape.
Photographs by Robert Edson Swain

FACING PAGE BOTTOM: Organic materials can often be highlighted with simple design solutions, such as this handcrafted pot.
Photograph by David M. Ohashi

"Landscape stewardship is forged through relationships and a philosophy that embraces value, quality, accountability and owner satisfaction."

—David M. Ohashi

ABOVE: Rich, bold use of materials responds to the challenge and effect of a floating platform that has minimum clearance to water level.
Photograph by David M. Ohashi

FACING PAGE: Successful definition of spaces, adjacent to entry, is accomplished through a water body that subtly separates yet unifies these spaces.
Photograph by Alex Hayden

KrisCo Aquatech Pools

Woodinville, Washington

"An artisan should never compromise on quality of workmanship."

—Bjarne Kristiansen

ABOVE: Throughout the years, KrisCo Aquatech Pools has gained critical experience in design, sharpening our skills to become one of the foremost pool builders in the Northwest. My hope is that our work enhances lifestyles, adding value to the home and family. So, a setting designed for privacy and solitude is ready for one to relax with a book.

FACING PAGE: The majority of our projects involve our teaming up with elite architecture, landscaping and construction firms to deliver the highest-quality product. Beauty and quality is delivered with integrity and reliability—for 25 years, we've been proud members of the Aquatech Society of Pool Builders and Retailers, the nation's largest society of pool professionals. Here, a peaceful place glows with radiance for those memorable moments of relaxation that carry across the infinity edge and the water of Puget Sound. How can one not relax?
Photographs by Kathy Muir

"Never shortcut something that could bite you later."

—Bjarne Kristiansen

ABOVE: The warm glow from inside the home spreads across the pool waters in the evening hours.

FACING PAGE TOP: Nature's landscape—an ageless beauty—seems to cross the infinity-edge water.

FACING PAGE BOTTOM: In the early evening, the majestic Mt. Rainier is mirrored in the still waters of the pool.
Photographs by Kathy Muir

"The idea is to create a functional product that is pleasing to the eye even when it's not in use."

—Bjarne Kristiansen

TOP & MIDDLE: Relax in your favorite chair to glance across Puget Sound with trickling water as your soundtrack. The magnitude of the views here never becomes tiring—truly a resort at home.

BOTTOM: The spa is located for privacy with water features spilling and fiber-optic lighting to add to the intimate atmosphere.

FACING PAGE: The family covets the uncommon setting and view. Their input and personal touch enhanced the yard, becoming a place where they can celebrate life.
Photographs by Kathy Muir

"Integrity in the ground, not seen, is just as important as what is seen above ground."

—Bjarne Kristiansen

ABOVE & FACING PAGE: Away from the hustle and busyness of life, the country-style personal haven can't be matched. The pool and spa were designed to fit the log home construction and natural setting. With Mt. Rainier in the background, the infinity-edge pool overlooks meadows, forest and a deer crossing.
Photographs by Kathy Muir

ABOVE & LEFT: The accomplished landscaping meets simplicity in the design of the pool and spa—both complementing the elegant home. The cabana, by the spa, has an outdoor barbecue kitchen.

FACING PAGE: It's the time of the day to take a dip in the pool or relax in the spa and watch through the mist of the waterfall glowing flames from the fire pit. To think that we helped make this a reality gives us great satisfaction.

Photographs by Kathy Muir

"I'm not there to build my shrine—we are there to build the owner's dream."

—Bjarne Kristiansen

CS Underground

Seattle, Washington

"Building with your eyes open—embracing problems and challenges—makes the project much more satisfying."

—Dorte Colella

ABOVE: This garden's multiple levels allowed for the creation of a variety of outdoor "rooms," each with its own unique design and ambience. The wood arbor and three-tiered fountain are surrounded by a hydrangeas garden and a dry-stack wall that frames the background.
Photograph by Mark Kihlstrom

FACING PAGE: The fire pit lounge area was built on the lowest tier of this garden in order to take advantage of the natural beauty of Puget Sound. Kenneth Philp Landscape Architects specified simulated rock and salt-tolerant plantings to create a lasting overall look.
Photograph by Steven Young Photography

"The level of perfection has to surpass the critical concept—if it were easy, anybody would do it."

—Joe Colella

ABOVE LEFT: The natural look of the granite stone in the hardscape design complements the home's exterior. The fraser firs provide the perfect natural screen at the property line, which was a narrow area, and enhance the Northwest feel of the garden.
Photograph by Mark Kihlstrom

ABOVE RIGHT: The tiered garden design features many colors and textures, such as lavender, Sedum, Weigela and daylilies. Keeping the lawn areas fresh and pristine was a challenge due to all the trades working on the residence for the Seattle Garden Tour.
Photograph by Mark Kihlstrom

FACING PAGE: Each autumn leaf granite paver was individually cut from imported granite slabs and placed to create the random design for this Puget Sound patio. Since the landscape was located on a critical slope area, bringing in all the necessary stone materials was a difficult test, not to mention the difficulty organizing cranes and gas-powered tract wheelbarrows, but the result was worth the effort.
Photograph by Steven Young Photography

"We truly are finishing the home—that's where the satisfaction lies."

—Mark Kihlstrom

ABOVE: This secluded side retreat of a Capitol Hill garden creates a serene walkway between the garden's lawn areas. In springtime, the Liburnum tree will have golden-yellow blooms, shaped similar to those of a wisteria vine, hanging down from the steel archway. The visual effect is both magical and elegant.
Photograph by Mark Kihlstrom

FACING PAGE TOP: The concrete bridge over a grotto water feature is the chief focal point of the entrance to the residence. The entry bridge was constructed utilizing a new application method of an existing concrete product to finish the vertical surfaces while a steel beam supports cast-in-place floating stair risers. Ostrich ferns, Brunnera Jack Frost, Japanese forest grass and Rodgersia were some of the grotto area plantings, which, along with the water feature, soften the industrial look of the bridge.
Photograph by Steven Young Photography

FACING PAGE BOTTOM: The granite stairs and pavers combined with scotch-moss ground cover and framed by hardy Fuchsia and wild ginger plantings create the look of the side stairway. Planting "green joints" between the pavers involves additional attention to the planting process while maintaining the equal spacing and even level of the sand-set pavers.
Photograph by Steven Young Photography

"The art of design is coaxing beauty from what exists."

—Susan Harrison

ABOVE & FACING PAGE: As a designer, I determine what the site needs and what the owners desire and craft spaces that overcome obstacles and are unique, each remarkable in its own way. The sculptural steel walls create a visual stop at the edge of the garden and act as a backdrop for irregular "mounds" of Japanese maples while screening unmanaged vegetation beyond without blocking distant views of the islands.
Photographs by Rod del Pozo

"It is the designer's job to foresee results."

—Susan Harrison

ABOVE: A deck railing had overlooked the need for access on this side of the house. The owners wanted something open and sculptural for this view. Sculptor Joe Clark of Architectural Elements and master carpenter Jim Hughes collaborated on this bronze and wood gate. The unusual triangular configuration of landing, railing and steps allowed access from two directions while directing outbound traffic away from a dangerous drop.

FACING PAGE TOP: A formalized meandering rill connects two fountains in an enclosed, paved courtyard. We carefully planned the zigzag rill to follow the random paving joints without creating awkward cutouts. It disappears and resurfaces.

FACING PAGE BOTTOM LEFT: The pedestrian path leading from the parking spaces to the front courtyard runs parallel to a disguised path, allowing small equipment access to the back of the house. The wild strawberry hides a compacted surface that will support several tons.

FACING PAGE BOTTOM RIGHT: The enclosing walls of the courtyard were intentionally left with a coarse finish—to expose the irregularities of the poured concrete—and stained the color of leaf tannin to highlight the plants in front of them. This is a garden example of wabi-sabi, the Japanese aesthetic of things beautifully imperfect.

Photographs by Rod del Pozo

"Working with architects and owners to find personal, one-of-a-kind solutions to create a beautiful garden is a wonderfully circular process."

—Susan Harrison

ABOVE: Modern permeable paving blends with traditional stonework for auxiliary parking away from the house. Access to the garden is through a stone arch.

FACING PAGE TOP LEFT: Proximity to the tea house encouraged continuation of an Asian influence for this way-stop on the path through the ravine. The Qrater by Belgian designer Dirk Wynants is a Cor-Ten steel fire dish designed to rust and was used here as a focal point for intimate gatherings away from the house.

FACING PAGE TOP & BOTTOM RIGHT: Sandstone from the site was augmented with similar stone quarried nearby and expertly assembled into walls and steps throughout the garden. The dry-laid sandstone retaining wall recycles the unearthed boulders from the house site. The lead mason was James Burr.

FACING PAGE BOTTOM LEFT: Tucked into a ravine behind the house, this little handcrafted building serves for ceremony and rest with hidden storage for gardening tools. Roof tiles and parts of the building originated in Japan.
Photographs by Rod del Pozo

ABOVE: A long, curving wall terminates in a stone-rimmed pool. As it reaches the pool, the top of the wall bends into the slope; the bottom of the wall plunges underwater. Water's components of reflection, moisture and sound are shaped and measured to create the best blended effect.

LEFT: As access for the gardener, cantilevered steps run up a stone retaining wall, inspired by European stone-wall stiles.

FACING PAGE TOP: We converted a space between the house and the garage into a Japanese-influenced courtyard with a potting shed for the owner—a bonsai hobbyist.

FACING PAGE BOTTOM: A nearby fishpond provided a hypothetical source for the waterspout over the antique stone basin.
Photographs by Rod del Pozo

"Crafting a great garden is harder than it looks. The articulation of the space must fit the character of those who live there."

—Susan Harrison

perspectives
ON DESIGN
pacific northwest

PACIFIC NORTHWEST TEAM
SENIOR ASSOCIATE PUBLISHER: Sharon Dedo
GRAPHIC DESIGNER: Ashley DuPree
EDITOR: Daniel Reid
PRODUCTION COORDINATOR: Drea Williams

HEADQUARTERS TEAM
PUBLISHER: Brian G. Carabet
PUBLISHER: John A. Shand
EXECUTIVE PUBLISHER: Phil Reavis
DIRECTOR OF DEVELOPMENT & DESIGN: Beth Benton Buckley
PUBLICATION & CIRCULATION MANAGER: Lauren B. Castelli
SENIOR GRAPHIC DESIGNER: Emily A. Kattan
GRAPHIC DESIGNER: Kendall Muellner
MANAGING EDITOR: Rosalie Z. Wilson
EDITOR: Anita M. Kasmar
EDITOR: Michael C. McConnell
MANAGING PRODUCTION COORDINATOR: Kristy Randall
PRODUCTION COORDINATOR: Laura Greenwood
PRODUCTION COORDINATOR: Maylin Medina
TRAFFIC COORDINATOR: Meghan Anderson
ADMINISTRATIVE MANAGER: Carol Kendall
ADMINISTRATIVE ASSISTANT: Beverly Smith
CLIENT SUPPORT COORDINATOR: Amanda Mathers

PANACHE PARTNERS, LLC
CORPORATE HEADQUARTERS
1424 Gables Court
Plano, TX 75075
469.246.6060
www.panache.com

Hensel Design Studios, page 203

index

THE PANACHE COLLECTION

CREATING SPECTACULAR PUBLICATIONS FOR DISCERNING READERS

Dream Homes Series
An Exclusive Showcase of the Finest Architects, Designers and Builders

Carolinas	Northern California
Chicago	Ohio & Pennsylvania
Coastal California	Pacific Northwest
Colorado	Philadelphia
Deserts	South Florida
Florida	Southwest
Georgia	Tennessee
Los Angeles	Texas
Metro New York	Washington, D.C.
Michigan	
Minnesota	
New England	
New Jersey	

Spectacular Homes Series
An Exclusive Showcase of the Finest Interior Designers

California	New York
Carolinas	Ohio & Pennsylvania
Chicago	Pacific Northwest
Colorado	Philadelphia
Florida	South Florida
Georgia	Southwest
Heartlands	Tennessee
London	Texas
Michigan	Toronto
Minnesota	Washington, D.C.
New England	Western Canada

Perspectives on Design Series
Design Philosophies Expressed by Leading Professionals

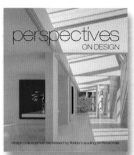

Carolinas	New England
Chicago	Pacific Northwest
Colorado	California
Florida	Southwest
Georgia	
Minnesota	

Art of Celebration Series
The Making of a Gala

New York
South Florida
Washington, D.C.

Spectacular Wineries Series
A Captivating Tour of Established, Estate and Boutique Wineries

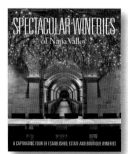

California's Central Coast
Napa Valley
New York
Sonoma County

Specialty Titles
The Finest in Unique Luxury Lifestyle Publications

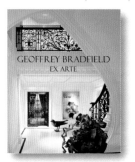

Distinguished Inns of North America
Extraordinary Homes California
Spectacular Golf of Colorado
Spectacular Golf of Texas
Spectacular Hotels
Spectacular Restaurants of Texas
Visions of Design
Geoffrey Bradfield Ex Arte
Cloth and Culture: Couture Creations of Ruth E. Funk
Into the Earth: A Wine Cave Renaissance

City by Design Series
An Architectural Perspective

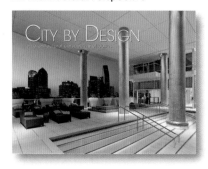

Atlanta
Charlotte
Chicago
Dallas
Denver
Orlando
Phoenix
San Francisco
Texas

PanacheDesign.com
Where the Design Industry's Finest Professionals Gather, Share and Inspire

PanacheDesign.com overflows with innovative ideas from leading architects, builders, interior designers and other specialists. A gallery of design photographs and library of advice-oriented articles are among the comprehensive site's offerings.

PANACHE PARTNERS, LLC • 1424 GABLES COURT • PLANO, TEXAS 75075 • 469.246.6060 • WWW.PANACHE.COM